Genealogical Data
THE SALEM TENTH
in West New Jersey

———o———

Compiled by

H. STANLEY CRAIG

———o———

Southern Historical Press, Inc.
Greenville, South Carolina

Originally Published 1926

All rights reserved. No part of this publication may be reproduced, stored in a retrieval system or transmitted in any form or by any means without the prior permission of the publisher.

SOUTHERN HISTORICAL PRESS, INC.
PO BOX 1267
Greenville, SC   29601

ISBN #978-1-63914-038-1

Printed in the United States of America

AUTHORITIES

* Pittsgrove Presbyterian Church Records.
† Salem Friends' Records.
‡ West Jersey Wills.
§ Salem Wills.
‖ Shourd's History of the Fenwick Colony.
¶ Marriage Records, New Jersey Archives.
†† Cushing & Sheppard's History of Gloucester, Salem and Cumberland Counties.
** Calendar of Wills, New Jersey Archives.
*** Cumberland Wills.

THE SALEM TENTH

Abbit, Abden, m Elizabeth Blew, 10-3-1745.*
Abdon, wf. Martha; chd. Benjamin, bap. 6-14-1747.*

Abbott, George, wf. Mary; chd. Benjamin, b 1-20-1699/1700; Hannah, b 9-30-1702; George, b 10-13-1704; Sarah, b 2-16-1706/7; Rebeckah, b 6-26-1709; Samuel, b 6-26-1712; Mary, b 8-26-1714.†
George, Elsenborough, will 3-18-1729, pr. 5-19-1729 ‡
John, cooper, noncupative will 3-9-1692/3, recorded 8-8-1729; wf. Elizabeth; bro. Thomas.§
Thomas, Cohansey, husbandman, will 12-14-1718, pr. 5-1-1719; wf. Margritt; chd. Mary, Ruth, Naomi; son Benoni Dare; bros. Stephen Abbot, George Abbot, Dickason Shepherd.‡
Samuel; wf. Hannah; chd. George, b 11-29-1734/5; William, b 4-4-1737, d 4th mo. 1800; Rebeckah, b 10-26-1740.†
Samuel m Hannah, dau. of Josiah and Amy Foster of Burlington county.‖

Acton, Benjamin, wf, Christiana; chd. Elijah, b 2-26-1690; Mary, b 10-17-1692; Benjamin, b 8-19-1695; Lydia , b 11-24-1697; Joshua, b 7-9-1700.†
Benjamin, wf. Elizabeth; chd. John, b 8-31-1728; Joseph, b 9-3-1730; Benjamin, b 9-15-1733; Benjamin, b 12-28-1735/6; Samuel, b 6-31-1738.†
Benjamin, Jr., tanner; wf. Elizabeth Hill.‖
Benjamin, Salem, tanner, will 11-18-1749; wf. wid. of William Sheals, by whom she has three daus.; sons, John and Joseph Acton.‡

Adams, Fenwick, Fenwicks Grove, will 6-7-1689, rec. 8-26-1689; wf. Ann.§
Fenwick, m Anne Watkins, 8-18-1687.¶
John, m Elizabeth, dau. John Fenwick; chd. Elizabeth, Fenwick, Mary.‡

Alderman, Thomas, Cohansey, weaver, will 8-13-1715, pr. 9-28-1715. Wf. Mary; chd. Thomas, Daniel, Mary, William.‡

William, wf. Abigail; chd. Tabitha, Susanna, Abigail, all bap. 8-10-1740; William, bap. 1-24-1741/2; Elizabeth, bap. 1-22-1743/4; Sarah, bap. 3-8-1745; Aaron, b 9-26-1747; Mary, b 1-14-1749/50.*

Aldridge, Hermann, Salem, m Sarah England, Philadelphia, 10-1-1733.¶

Alen, John, m Mary Huckings, 8-10-1686.¶

Alewell (Elweall), **Thomas, Sr.,** Pilesgrove Precinct, will, 4-25-1706, pr. 4-26-1707; carpenter; wf. Sarah; chd. Sarah Walling, Mary Nicholds, Elizabeth Alewell, Thomas, William, John, Samuel.‡

Alexander, Joseph, Cohansey, wf. Rachel refused admx. 12-23-1726.**

Robert, Cohansey, inv. of estate 1-27-1727/8.**

Alldricks, Euard, Penns Neck, will 7-15-1696; wf Elizabeth; chd Allderix Euertson, Armeniah Alldricks.§

Allen, Ebenezer, will 9-18-1716; wf. Mary; bros. Samuel and Thomas Allin; sister, Mindwell Holton; cousins, Ebenezar Miller and Thomas Alexander (all of the above relations living in Northampton, Hampshire county, New England); wife's children, Thomas, William, Mary and Daniel Alderman (all under age); pr. 12-26-1716.‡

Ephraim, Alloways Creek, will 8th day 9th month (Nov,) 1726, pr. 2-21-1726/7. Wf. Hannah; chd. James, Benjaman, Joseph, Isack (under age), Uesty Powel, with whom Aubitha Allen is to live until 16.‡

Isaac, blacksmith, Alloways Creek, int. 2-20-1739. Wf. Mary.‡
Jane, came in Griffith, as servant of Christopher White, 1675.††
John, husbandman, inv. 22d day 9th month (Nov.) 1697.§
John, bond of adm. of estate, 1-4-1702/3; wf. Rebecca.§

Anderson, Simon. Wf. Hester; son Thomas b 5-25-1702.†

Angelo, Charles, m Katharine Knox, 10-6-1690.¶

Ashbury, Ebenezer, m Margaret Deffose, 7-19-1694.¶
Hannah, came in 1681.‖

Attwood, Jacob, Manenton, carpenter, w 7-28-1742, pr. 2-23-1744. Wf. Christian; bro. Abraham Attwood who has son John; neice Susannah Lord (widow) dau of Abraham Attwood.‡

Austen, Cornelius, Cumberland Co., int. 5-16-1748. Wf. Martha.‡
Martha, int. 10-19-1748. Wid. of Cornelius.‡

Austin, Edward, Philadelphia, m Sarah Weatherby, Salem, 5-6-1748.¶

Ayars, Stephen, Cohansey. will 2-27-1725/6, pr. 4-12-1726. Mother, Hester Ayers; bros. John, Joshua, Caleb and Robert.‖

Ayers, John, Cohansey, will 12-21-1740, pr. 4-24-1741. Wf. Secily; chd. Samuel, John, Mary, Steven.‡

Robert, Cohansey, will 2-25-1716/17. Wf. Esther; chd. Isaac who has son Caleb; Juda, Caleb, Robert, John, Esther wf. of John Garm.‡

Ayres, Isaac, weaver, formerly of Easthampton, Suffolk Co., N. Y., int. 11-5-1744. Bros. Benjamin Erys, Jr. and William Erys; sisters, Clemens Erys and Elizabeth Domony wf. of Nathaniel Domony, Jr., of Easthampton ‡

Bacon, Abel, Bacon's Neck, Cohansie, will, 12-14-1733. Wf; Mercy; chd. William and Sarah; mother-in-law Mary Bacon.‡

Jeremiah, Salem, sadler. will 8-1-1731, pr. 8-9-1731. Chd. Hannah. Lettisha and Nathaniel; bro.-in-law Richard Wood.**

Jeremiah, inv. 1-11-1747/8.‡

John, Cohansey, will 12-8-1715, pr. 12-17, 19 and 29, 1715. Wf. Grace; chd. John, Edmond, Job and Lucy. all under age.**

John. Wf. Elizabeth; chd. Thomas, b 6-29-1721; John, b 11-30-1724; Elizabeth, b 10-21-1726; David, b 1-14-1729; Martha, b 5-4-1731; Mary, b 8-17-1733; Job, b 10-16-1735.†

John, m Elizabeth Smith, 10-17-1688.¶

Joseph, m Elizabeth Pancoast, 8-11-1693.¶

Joseph. Wf. Margaret; chd. Edmund, b 12-12-1725; Esther, b 7-23-1735; Margaret, b 2-20-1737; Deborah, b 10-22-1733; Joseph, b 10-22-1733; Prudence, b 12-27-1744; Richard, b 12-24-1746; Samuel, b 5-20-1747; Jesse, b 5-23-1749; Elizabeth, b 5-30-1751.†

Joseph, Cohansey, m Margaret Hancock, Alloway, 2-5-1733.†

Martha, wid., will 5-6-1697, rec. 4-3-1700. Chd. Samuel, Joseph, Ann Gillman, Nat., Jeremiah, William.§

Nathaniel, Cohansey, will 5-25-1701, rec. 2-4-1702/3. Wf. Katherine; chd. Nathaniel, Jeremiah, Lydia, all under age; bros.. Jona. Holmes and William Bacon.§

Nathaniel, Cohansey, cooper, will 3-8-1725/6, pr. 4-11-1726. Wf. Rebacha.‡

Samuel, int. 2-6-1740. Hannah Bacon, adm.‡

Samuel, Sr., int. 1-25-1747.‡

Thomas Wf. Elener; chd. Charles, b 1-13-1748; Rachel, b 10-20-1756; Dorcas, b 8-20-1758.†

William. Cohansey, will 1-8-1725/6, pr. 2-26-1725/6. Wf. Mary; chd. Abell, Mary, Isaac, Rachel, Jacob, Nathan, Anna, Sarah Wallen, William, Hannah Wallford.‡

Bagley, Charles, Cohansey, tanner, will 4-15-1699, rec. 4-2-1700. Wf. Elizabeth; chd. Jean, Sarah, Charles (under age); cousins Elizabeth Jean and Mary Jean; son-in-law Thomas Craven.§

Bailie, David, Salem, waterman, adm. of estate, 7-2-1723. Wf. Sarah.‡

Baitman, John, Cohansey, inv of estate 3-10-1725/6. Wf. Rebeca.‡

Bakon (Bacon), **Benjamin,** Cohansey, blacksmith, inventory 5-6-1714.§

Baldwin, Thomas, and wf. came from England in 1683.††

Barker, Aquilla. Wf. Mary; chd. Thomas, b 1-23-1706/7; Hannah, b 9-25-1708; Aquilla, b 10-4-1710; John, b 12-14-1712; Daniel, b 12-2-1714; Samuel, b 12-16-1716; Abraham, b 11-16-1718; Isaac, b 1-22-1720/21; Jacob d 4-4- 1765.†

Aquilla. Wf. Hannah; children, Hannah, b 1-12-1739; Susannah, b 1-28-1741; Sarah, b 6-4-1744; Liddy, b 1-22-1746; Aquilla, b 5 17-1749; James, b 2-13-1752.†

Jacob. Wf. Rebeckah; chd. David, b 9-16-1747; Jonathan; b 1-3-1750; Elijah, b 10-29-1750; Louisa, b 11-13-1754.†

John, Pilesgrove, will 12-30-1720, pr. 11-29-1721. Wf. Elizabeth; chd. Benjamin (under age), Elizabeth, Anna, and Phebee.‡

Nathaniel, Quahoken. Wf. Jane; chd. Joseph, bap. 9-30-1743.

Samuel, Pilesgrove, int. 12-13-1740.‡

Barcleson, John, int. 11-14-1744.‡

Barker, Wade, m Hannah Stretch, dau. of Bradway and Sarah. Chd. Hannah, m 1st Robert Watson, 2d James Sayres. ||

William, m Elizabeth Gregory, 1-7-1739.¶

Barnes, Patience, south side of Cohansey, wid., will 12-27-1716. pr. 1-12-1716/17. Chd. Joshua, Temperance Wick, Sarah Sayre, Samuel; son-in-law Anthony Ludlam, husband of deceased daughter Patience.‡

Samuel, m Sarah Hollingshead 5-20-1738.¶

Baron, (Barrow) **Zachariah,** Greenwich. cordwinder, will 7-30-1725, pr. 4-18-1726. Mother-in-law Mary Field.‡

Barracliff, John, m Prudence Bradway 3-7-1747.†

Barrat, Prudence, Salem Town, inv. (?)-23-1725/6.§

Barrall, Thomas, Mannington Twp., will 4-9-1733, pr. 5-10-1733. Wf Elizabeth; chd. Thomas, Rachel, Elizabeth and Quinn (all under age).‡

Barrett, James, Sr., Mannington Precinck, carpinture, will 8-12-1717, pr 11-15-1717. Wf. Elizabeth; chd. James, Thomas, Caleb, William, Elizabeth (last two under age)‡

Bartleson, (Barkleson) **Andrew,** Fenwicks Grove, planter, will 9-17-1690, rec. 12-12-1691. Wf. Katherine; chd. 3 sons and dau. Katherine.§

Andrew, Penns Neck, int. 2-26-1747. Wf. Sarah.**

John, husbandman, will 4-18-1723. Wf. Gunnlo (?).‡

William, Mannington, int. 3-26-1750. Sarah Bartleson, his adm., m Jeremiah Baker of Penns Neck.**

Zachariah, Penns Neck, inv. 4-28-1729. Adm. Sarah Bartleson.‡ and §.

Barton, Enoch, cordwinder, non will 7-1-1709.§

Basker, Joseph, wool comber, int. 4-29-1734.‡

Bassett, Benjamin, will 11-9-1726, pr. 4-27-1727. Bro. William Bassett.‡

Daniel, Pilesgrove, will 9-19-1745, inv. 11-2-1745. Wf. Mary; chd. Daniel, Zebedee, Elizabeth, Hannah, Sarah, Mary, Amy.‡

Elisha, son of William, came with his father from Boston in 1691; located near Woodstown.††

Elisha, son of William, m Abigail Elizabeth, dau. of John and Dorothea Davis of Pilesgrove. Chd. Sarah, b 1719, m Thomas Smith of Mannington; Elizabeth, b 23d of 2d month, 1720, m Thomas Davis; Elisha, b 12-15-1722; Davis, b 1725; Samuel, b 1728; Rebecca, m John Page; Rachel, b 1736, m Andrew Miller; Isaac.‖

William, migrated from Massachusetts in 1691 and settled near Salem.††

William, Pilesgrove, will 22d of 2d month (April) 1729, pr. 10-25-1733. Wf. Rebeckah.‡

Bateman, John, m Sarah Luptin, 8-21-1746.¶

Bayley, David, Salem Town, inv. 1-1-1722/3. Wf. Sarah.**

Bedford, Gunning, (Gunnion, Gunian), Penns Neck, inv. 2-8-1724/5. Wf. Mary.‡

Beere, Jonathan, Salem, gent., will 7-30-1701. Wf. Mary.§

Beetil, (Beetles) **George,** Alloways Creek, will 2-27-1713/14. Uncle Josiah White; aunt Hannah White.‡

Bell, John, Morrisses River, Cumb. Co., will 2-18-1749, pr. 6-20-1749. Wf. Mary; chd. John, Henry, Robert, Mary, Agnes.‡

Bender, Robert, Greenwich Twp., Cumb, Co., bond of adm. 8-25-1749. Wf. Susanna.***

Bennet, Robert, Cohansey Precinct, husb., inv. 3-2-1703/4. Wf. Jane.**

Beriman, (Baryman, Bereman), **Thomas,** Cohansey, will 3-7-1746/7, pr. 6-14-1749. Wf. Martha; chd. Annabel Johnson, Rachel, Benet, Parthenia Reeves, Elizabeth, Zurviah and Hannah (last three under age).‡

Beswick, Ephraim, inv. 1-15-1710/11.**
John, bricklayer, will 12-7-1699. Sons Ephraim and John.§

Bilderback Albert, Penns Neck, husb., will 4-6-1728, pr. 5-5-1732. Wf. Margaret; chd. Daniel, Peter, John (under age), Sarah. Jane, Margaret (under age); bro.-in-law Sicink Sinickson.‡
David, will rec. 7-10-1695. Wf. Katherine; chd. Hendrick, John, Peter, Katherine (all under age).§
Peter, int. 4-3-1740. Wf. Sarah.§
Peter, Penns Neck, husb., will 5-22-1700, inv. 4-10-1701; Wf. Ingra; chd. Daniel, Albert, Katherine, Ann.§

Bishop, Abigail, wid., Hopewell Twp., Cumb. Co, int. 7-4-1749.***

Daniel, Cohansey, will 3-19-1742/3, pr. 4-30-1743. Wf. Abigail; chd. Nathan. Daniel, Elizabeth, Phebe (last three under age).‡
Moses. Hopewell Twp., Cumb. Co., will 6-12-1749, pr. 7-8-1749. Chd. Moses, Levi, Esther. Mary, Rachel Eunice (daus. under age).‡
Nathaniel, Cohansey, will 5-9-1720, pr. 5-28-1723. Wf. Sarah; chd. Daniel Joseph, Moses, Nathaniel, Samuel, John and three daus. not named.‡
Nathaniel, Cohansey, will 3-6-1748/9, pr. 4-1/1749. Wf. Mary; chd. Isaac, Preston. Jeremiah, Zephaniah, Nathaniel, Mary Lupton, Abigail, Elizabeth, Hannah.‡
Samuel. Wf. Mary; chd. John, bap. 1-31-1741/2; Naomi, bap. 5-15-1743; Mary, bap. 8-12-1744; Sarah, bap. 4-27-1746; Samuel, bap. 9-4-1748.*

Blackfield, Ann, wf. of Peter, Salem Town, dau. of Samuel Curtise, will 12-5-1703, pr. 12 29-1703.§
Peter, Salem Town, late of New England, marriage contract with Ann Gill, wid.; dau. of Samuel Curtise.**

Blanchard, Philip, Alloways Creek, will 5-16-1743, pr. 5-20-1743. Sister Elizabeth, wf. of Joseph Ware; bro.-in-law Jeremiah Powell who has chd. John, Elizabeth and Mary.‡

Blin, John, Wf. Elizabeth; chd. Ann, bap. 5-24-1741.*

Boggs, Samuel, m Rebecca Boggs, 1-18-1730.¶

Booth, James, Hopewell Twp., Cumb. Co., weaver, will 1-24-1748/9, pr. 2-2-1748. Sisters Issable Booth, Agness McClong, Esther McMungall, Margaret Wood, Elizabeth Nealy; cousin John Nealy (under age), son of Joseph Nealy.‡

Richard. Wf. Ann; chd. Richard, b 3-21-1739; Elizabeth, b 2-14-1742; Ruth, b 5-15-1746; Sarah, b 9-25-1748·†

Boorows (Burrows), **Edward,** Cohansey, nv. 2-18-1729/30.§

Boon, Andrew, Penns Neck, will 2-27-1739/40, affirmed 6-4-1740 Chd. Peter, Andrew; Tobias, Cornelius, dau. Garter; bro. Peter Boon.‡

Peter, Penns Neck, will 1-7-1748/9, pr. 4-5-1749   Grandfather Cornelius Corneliuson.‡

Peter, will 1733, pr. 7-27-1733: Son Peter; mother Catherin Savoy; brother Andrew Boon.‡

Peter, Penns Neck, will 3-29-1707, pr. 11-18-1707. Wf. Bekceketere.‡ Inv. sworn to by Catherine Boon, executrix.§

Bowen, Dan, Cohansey, will 2-5-1728/9, pr. 4-25-1729. Wf. Mary; chd. Mary, Enoch, Noah, Eve, Deborah, Phecb, Elijah (all under age), Dan and Jonathan; bro. John Walling.‡

Isaac, Fairfield Precinct, Cumb. Co., will 1748, pr. 9-2-1748. Wf. Phebe; chd. Clephon, Isaac (both under age), Phebe, Esther, Susannah.‡

John, Cohansey, will 10-12-1747, pr. 11-30-1747. Wf. Rachel; chd. Joseph, Samuel, Isaac, John, James, Lidya, Joana, Abigail, Hannah, William; son-in-law Neihemia Hoggbon ‡

Richard, int. 4-18-1735. Wf. Mary.‡

Samuel, Jr , Cohansie, carpenter, will 12-19-1727, pr. 5-1-1728. Wf. Martha; chd. Samuel, Stephen, Siles, Nathaniel, Cataran, Moses (all under age); bros. Elijah Bowen and James Dixon.‡

Samuel, Cohansey, gent., will 1-21-1728/9. Chd. John, Dan, Elijah, Clefton, Mary Perey and Elizabeth Fogg.‡

Samuel, Cohansey, int. 2-10-1742. Wf. Martha.‡

Bowers, Ebenezer, m Prisilla Burrows (?), 5-1-1730.¶

Bowin, George. m Charity Davis, 8-26-1738.¶

Boyer, Arthur, Alloways Creek, sadler, will 11-7-1730, affirmed 12-22-1731. Sisters Mary, wf. of William Smith; Elizabeth, wf of Hugh Clifton; Martha, wf. of Gabriel Wood: bro. William Smith.‡

James, inv. 3-11-1694/5. Wf. Elizabeth.‡

Bradford, William, husb., will 9-11-1747, pr. 3-25-1747. Wf. Mary; chd. Reymond (dau.), William (both under age); son-in-law Benjamin Parvin.‡

Brading, Nathaniel, Salem Town, merchant, will 1-4-1712/13, pr. 2-19-1712/3. Wf. Sarah.§

Bradshaw, Lemuel, husb., died int. 13th day, 11th mo. (January), 1689/90.§

Bradway, Aaron. Wf. Mary; chd. Rebecca. b 7-19-1743; Joshua, b 9-9-1748 O. S.†

Aaron, m Mary Walden, 10-10-1742.¶

Aaron, m first, Sarah; chd. Joshua, Sarah, wf. of Johathan Waddington. He m second, Sarah Smith, wid. of John Smith of Amblebury; chd. Thomas. He m third, Widow Rolph; chd. Hannah R., m David Bradway.‖

Edward, of Parish of Paul Chadwell, London, with wf. Mary. daus. Mary and Susannah, and servants William Groome, Francis Burkell and John Alinn arrived in West Jersey, at Salem, 7th mo. 1677. Other chd. Sarah, b 7-27-1677; Hannah, b 7-17-168-.†

Edward, Munmouth River, will 12-6-1693, pr. 4-14-1694. Wf. Mary; chd. William who has a son Edward, Susannah, Sarah, Hannah (last three under age); grandson John son of William Cooper. Codicil 3-16-1693/4 mentions dau. Mary Kenton.§

John, Alloways Creek Precinct, cordwainer, will 6-3-1739, pr. 8-25-1739. Wf. Mary; chd. John and Hannah; bro. William Clark.‡

Jonathan, m 1st, Mary, dau. of Jonathan Daniels, Sr.; chd. William, b 1728; Rachel and Jonathan. 2d wf. Susanna, dau. of Charles Oakford, Jr;. chd. Edward, b 1741; Sarah and Nathan.‖

Jonathan. Wf. Mary; chd. William, b 7-13-1728; Rachel, b 1-11-1735; Jonathan, b 7-17-1735; Edward, b 3-31-1741; Sarah, b 7-28-1743; Nathan, b 2-15-1746.†

Joshua, miller, int. 12-7-1748.‡

Joshua, m Hannah Wiggins, 3-8-1739.¶

Mary, wid., Munmouth River, alias Alloways Creek, will 8th d. 6th mo. (August), 1696, rec. 9-1-1696. Chd Hannah Bradway, Mary Middleton, Sarah Hall and William Bradway.§

Susannah, Munmouth River, spinster, coheiress with William Bradway, Sarah wf. of William Hall, carpenter, of Salem; and Hannah Bradway. Adm. granted to Hugh Middleton and his wf. Mary, 9-13-1696.§

William. Wf. Elizabeth; chd. Sarah, b 1-29-1660; Edward, b 8-28-

1692; William, b 11-21-1695; Jonathan, b 1-22 1698/9, d 3d mo. 1765; Elizabeth, b 1-16-1700/1.†

William, eldest son of Edward, m in 1691, Elizabeth, b in London in 1669, dau. ot Christopher White. Chd. Edward, b 1692; William, b 1699; Elizabeth, b 1701, m Fenwick Adams ‖

William, Stow Creek, gent., will 5-3-1710, pr. 6-2-1710. Wf. Patience; chd. William, Edward (eldest son), Jonathan, John, Mary and Elizabeth.‡

William, b 1728, son of Jonathan, m Sarah Hancock. Chd. Admy, William, and Mary wf. of John Thompson ot Elsinborough.‖

Braeding, James, Cesaria River, late of Boston, Mass., merchant, non. will 11-9-1701; adm. granted to bro. Nathaniel Brading, merchant, Boston, 5-23-1702.§

Bragg, Roger, schoolmaster, int. 8-21-1739.‡

Braithwaite, Joane, wid., will 1-24-1697/8. Son-in-law (? stepson) William Braithwaite; son Manning Braithwaite; cousin John Worlidge; sister-in-law Ester Dun; rec.1-13-1701/2.§

Manning, inv. 2-17-1702/3. Wf. Margaret §

William, Sr., gent., Mannington Creek, non. will 3-13-1689/90, rec. 4-26-1690. Wf. Joane; chd. William and Manning.§

William, inv. 6-7-1712.**

William, m Ann Worlidge, 7-2-1702.¶

Braman (Brayman), **John,** Cohansey, will 5-31-1726. Wf. Catherine; chd. Daniel and Joseph; cousin Samuel Bowen; pr. 6-10-1726.‡

Braven, Newcomb, mariner, int. 5-23-1743. Wf. Mary Ann.‡

Brice, John, int. 5-25-1740.‡

Brick, John, Greenwich Meeting. Wf. Ann; chd. Mary, b 2-10-1730; Elizabeth, b 3-4-1732; John, b 11-10-1733; Joseph, b 3-24-1735; Ann, b 1-23-1738; Hannah, b 3-3-1741, d 4-22-1766; Ruth, b 10-1-1742; Jean, b 3-10-1743.†

John, Jr., d 23d day 1st mo. 1758, m Ann, dau. of Abel and Mary (Tyler) Nicholson; chd Mary, m Nathaniel Hall of Mannington; Elizabeth, m John Reeve; John; Joseph, m 1st Rebecca Abbott, 2d Martha Reeve; Ann, m Joseph Clement; Hannah; Ruth, m 1761, Benjamin Reeve; Jane.‖

Joseph, m Elizabeth Cairle, 4-1.1736.¶

Joshua, m Ruth Ramsey, 7-25-1737.¶

William, m Rachel Dare, Cumberland, 6-1-1731.¶

Brinton, Thomas, came in the Griffith as servant of Christopher White.††

Broockes (Brooks), **Timothy, Sr.,** will 3-12-1708/9, pr. 10-7-1712. Wf. Mahittebell, chd. Josiah, John, Timothy, daus not named; son-in-law Jonathan Kingsber.**

Brookes, Timothy, will 5-29-1730, pr. 4-1-1731. Son Timothy; bro. Zebulon.‡

Brooks, Henry, Deerfield, will 2-18-1749/50, pr.,3-5-1749. Chd. Henry, Joel, Mahattalle and Lydia; bro. Josiah Brooks.‡

John, Deerfield Twp., int. 7-7-1749.***

Josiah, Cohansey, inv. 4-25-1732. Wf. Lucy.§

Josiah, Cohansey, int. 6-8-1732 Wf. Lucy.‡

Josiah, Fairfield Twp., Cumb. Co., int. 3-11-1750. Abigail Brooks, adm.‡

Timothy, Cohanze, will 1-26-1715/6, pr. 2-10-1715/16. Wf. Hannah; chd. Seath, Timothy, Zebelon, Hannah, Patience, Kesiah, Zeuriah.**

Timothy, d int; bond of adm. 6-5-1730.**

Zebulon, Cohansey, will 3-7-1744/5, pr. 2-3-1748. Wf. Esther; chd. John, Zebulon, Mary, James (under age).‡

Broomfield, (Bloomfield, Brumfield) **William,** Alloways Creek, will 11-6 1713, pr. 6-23-1714. Chd. William, Elizabeth and Mary‡

Brown, James, Wf. Elizabeth; chd. Joseph, b 3-30-1730.†

John, int. 1-24-1735. Wf. Johannah.

John. Chd. Isaac, bap. 7-20-1746.*

Mathew, Pilesgrove, int. 9-21-1741.†

Thomas, Cohansey, will 3-14-1725/6, pr. 4-21-1726. Wf. Anna; chd. Thomas (under age); John, Abraham, Elizabeth and Anna (last two under age).‡

Browne, Joseph, Cesaria River, Merchant, will 3-25-1711, pr. 9-3-1711. Wf. Martha; chd. Isaac (under age) and Hannah.**

Bryant, William, int. 9-20-1749.‡

Buck, Ephraim, Cohansey, weaver, will 4-17-1738, pr. 6-15-1738. Wf. Ruth; chd. Ephraim, Joseph and Abigail (all under age); bro. Henry Buck, who has dau. Hannah (under age).‡

Henry, blacksmith, son of Henry Buck of Wethersfield, Conn., came to Cohansey previous to 1702 and settled in Back Neck.††

Henry, Esq., Fairfield, will 2-9-1725/6, pr. 2-21-1725/6. Wf. Rachel; chd. Henry, Ephraim, Jeremiah, Daitton and Judah.‡

Henry, Cohansey, will 3-14-1725/6, pr. 4-18-1726. Wf. Ruth; chd. Henry, Jane and Hannah.**

Buckley, Francis, husb., Munmouth River, inv. 31st day of 8th

mo. (Oct.), 1696. Adm. granted to Wf., Ann.§
  Grace, wid., Penns Neck, int., 4-26-1748.‡
  Richard, Penns Neck, adm. 9-1-1722. Wf. Katherine.‡
  Thomas, husb., Elsinburg, will 1-24-1721/2, pr. 1-4-1722/3.‡

Bulfin, Thomas, int. 10-19-1750.‡

Bull, Andrew, m Prudence Morris, 1-24-1745.¶
Bully, Edward, m Ann Brooks, 12-3-1736.¶

Burgin (Burgen), **John,** Cohansey, will 5-28-1737, pr. 6-24-1737. Wf. Margaret; chd. Joseph, John and Philip (all under age).‡
  John, m Margate Steele, 7-31-1728.¶
  Joseph, m Jane Silver, 3-23-1691/2.¶
  Joseph, will 1-30-1707/8, pr. 7-15-1709. Wf. Jane; son John; other chd. not named.‡

Burgrave, John, cooper, Penns Neck, inv. 3-19-1702/3. Wf. Elizabeth.‡

Burrell, Moses, Salem, will rec. 6-24-1689. Wf. Darcus; chd. Moses and Elizabeth.§
  Moses, inv. 2-18-1716/17.**

Burroughs, Edward, adm. granted Priscilla Burroughs, 7-20-1730.†
  William, mariner, int. 4-28-1743. Wf. Sarah.‡

Burwell, Moses. Wf. Dorcas; chd. Moses, b 6-20-1695, at Lynn, New England.†

Butcher, John, Stow Creek, will 11-12-1726, pr. 12-12-1726. Wf. Jane; son James, b 2-10-1726.‡ and †
  Richard, Cohansey, will 2-21-1715/16, pr 3-7-1715/16. Wf. Ann; chd. Margaret, Richard, John, Mary, Elizabeth, Hannah (last five under age) **

Butterwert, James, Penns Neck, will 11-27-1748, pr. 12-3-1848. Wf. Katherine; chd. James, Elinor; Francis and Katherine.§
  James, int. 8-26-1750.‡

Buttler, John, inv. 7-15-1709.‡
  Stephen, Alloways Creek Precinct, will 3-14-1721/2. pr. 4-16-1623 Bro. John Buttler of Coventry, Eng.; sister Mary of Coventry; bro.-in-law Isaac Biskar.‡

Caams, John Leonard, m Margaret Hea, 2-23-1748.¶

Callahan (Kalehan), **John,** farmer, Penns Neck, will 2-24-1749/50, pr. 9-3-1750. Wf. Margrat; chd. Marey, John and Margrat.‡

Cam, John. Wf. Mary; chd. Jenet, bap. 6-5-1748.*

Campbell, Charles, m Jane McKnight, 12-1-1732.¶

Canada, Jane, Alloways Creek; chd. James and Patrick, bap. 8-13-1747.*

Canton, William, sawyer, Elsenburrough, will 4-20-1716, pr. 5-10-1716.**

Carary, Roger, Salem, will 3-5-1692/3, rec. 7-6-1693. Wf. Elizabeth; chd. Rachel and Mary; sisters Elizabeth Goose and Dea.§

Roger, s of Christopher and Margaret of County Devon, Eng., was b in Ratcliffe Street, Bristol, County Somerset, Eng., 3-3-1651; at abt. the age of 21 he removed to Ireland, and after five years m Elizabeth Stephenson, dau. of John and Mary, both of Eng., who had removed to Ireland. In 1681 he removed to West Jersey in "The Owners' Adventure," arriving at Elsinburgh 9-10-1681. Chd. Rachel, b in Dublin 1680; and Mary, b at Salem 12-22-1685.†

Carle, John. Wf. Catherine; chd. John, bap. 5-6-1744; Rachel, bap. 11-30-1746; Abraham, bap. 4-26-1748/9.*

Sarah, wid., int. 3-14-1739.‡

Carll, Abiel, Sr., int. 3-17-1739.‡

Carney, Thomas, b in Ireland 1709, emig. abt. 1725; m Hannah, dau. John Proctor of Penns Neck. He d 1784; Hannah his wf. d 1778. Chd. Thomas and Peter.††

Carpenter, Preston. Wf. Hannah; chd. Hannah, b 10-4-1743, m Jedediah Allen, Jr.; William, b 10-1-1754, d 1-12-1837.†

Carrol, Patrick, m Elizabeth McCarty, 9-15-1741.*

Carruthers, James, Salem, m Lydia Roberts, Cohansie, 12-6-1733. Bond of adm. 12-24-1747 ¶ and ‡

Carter, William, Fairfield Twp., int. 12-26-1749.***

Cartwright, Robert, husb., inv. 10th mo. (Dec.), 29th d. 1702. Wf. Ann.§

Casbey, Bradway, ward, son of Edward and Elizabeth, of Salem, 1-8-1744.‡

Case, Thomas, inv. 12th d, 3d mo. (May), 1729 Elizabeth Case, adm.‡ and §

Casparson (Casperson), **Anthony,** m Elizabeth Redstreak, 10-15-1739.¶

Johannes, Penns Neck, will 11-14-1733, pr. 1-28-1733/4. Chd. John, **Susannah,** Catren Enlowes, Marey Boerd, Rebecca, Tobias and

Anthony.‡
Tobias, int. 4-30-1734. Wf. Judith,‡

Chambless, James, Jr. Wf. Mary; chd. James, b 28th d of 1st mo., 1721.†
James, int. 2-12-1750.‡
James, s of James and Mary, m Mary Fetters. Chd. Sarah, m William Smith; Mary, m David Smith; Rebecca.‖
Nathaniel (originally Chamness), and s, Nathaniel, came in the ship Griffith.††
Nathaniel. Wf. Eleanor; chd. James, b 22d of 1st mo., 1689; Mary, b 1692; Elizabeth, b 1700; Hannah, b 1702; Nathaniel, 3d, b 1705.‖
Nathaniel, 3d, m Susan, dau. Wade Oakford. Chd. Sarah, m William, s of John Hancock.‖

Chamless, James, Alloways Creek, inv, 24th of 10th mo. (Dec.), 1729. Hannah Chamless, adm.**

Chamness, James, Wf. Mary; chd. Rebecca, b 11-3-1716; Mary, b 6-3-1719; James, b 3-29-1721.†
James. Wf. Margaret; chd. Elizabeth, b 5-10;1723.†
Nathaniel. Wf. Elenor; chd. James, b 1-21-1689; Mary, b 11-12-1692.†
Nathaniel. Wf. Rebeckah; chd. Elizabeth, b 9-30-1700; Hannah, b 9-16-1702; Nathaniel, b 2-7-1705.†

Champleys, Edward, joiner in England, m Priscilla, eldest dau. of John Fenwick in 1671 at Reading, Eng.; came to Salem in "Griffith." Priscilla d 1683; Edward d 1706.††

Champness, Edward, int. 1-22-1732. Bro. Fenwick Champness.‡
Nathaniel, Alloways Creek, will 20th of 7th mo (Sept.), 1717. Chd. James, Mary Evens, Nathaniel, Elizabeth and Hannah Pr. 1-10-1725/6.‡ and §

Champneys, Edward, inv. 12-23-1707. Son John.‡
Joseph (Chamles, Chamness), Piles Grove Precinct, will July 1715, pr. Sept. 28, 1715. Wf Merrion; chd. Joseph; sister Lizabeth and John Whitehall who have a s William; cousin Roger Hudgins.**
Nathaniel (Champnes), Sr., Alloways Creek, will 13th of 12th mo. (Feb.), 1698, rec. 11-18-1700. Wf. Elizabeth; chd. Nathaniel, and Mary Hancock; grandchd. Mary Champneys, James Champneys, and Elizabeth Hancock.§
Nathaniel. Wf. Susannah; chd. Hannah, b 8-4-1738; Rebecca, b 4-9-1742.†
William, Millbrook, adm. 9-22-1701. Bro. Joseph Champneys.§

Chanders, James, Anns Grove, carpenter, will 12-20-1709, pr. 2-8-1709/10. Mother Frances Godwinn; bros. Robert Bonewell of Philadelphia and Samuel Chanders.‡

Chandler, John, blacksmith, Greenwich, will 2-16-1727/8, pr. 12-16-1728. Wf. Christian; chd. Samuel, John, Jacob, Ruth, Rachel, Sarah (all under age).‡
  Joseph, int. 1-29-1732. Mary Chandler, adm.**
  Samuel, inv. 6-1-1728.**

Chanillor, William, smith, Salem Town, inv. 6-6-1718. Wf. Rachel.‡

Chatfield, John, Cohansey, will 9-10-1717, pr. 4-1-1721. Sons Daniel (under age) and Thomas Brown. Five daus. not named.‡

Chetwood, Phillip, physician, will 7-17-1745, pr. 7-29-1745. Son John, (under age); bro. William Chetwood; sister-in-law Elizabeth Hall.

Clark, Thomas, s of George, b 1742, m Deborah, dau. of Thomas Denny, and located near Auburn. Son George.††

Clarke, William, Fairfield, husb., Inv. 3-27-1702. Wf. Patience.§

Clifton, Hugh. Wf. Elizabeth; chd. William, b 10-31-1737; Joseph, b 12-26-1730; Mary, b 4-17-1731.†

Close, John, Deerfield Precinct, int. 4-1-1749. Wf. Elinor.‡

Coaksley, William, Elsinburgh, merchant, inv. 13th of 4th mo. (June), 1721.**

Coale (Cole), **Cornelius,** Cohansey, gent., will 3-10-1725/6, pr. 5-21-1726. Wf. Catherine; daus.-in-law (?step-daughters) Lidia and Hope.‡

Coats, Thomas, weaver, int. 1-281-733.‡

Cock, Peter, Gloucester, m Beata Lock, Salem, 1-5-1738.¶

Cole, Thomas, husb. Elizabeth Cole, adm., 4-23.1729.‡

Coleman, Joseph, Salem, merchant, will 1-21-1727/8, pr. 8-15-1732. Wf Mary; chd. Ann, Mary, Elizabeth, Rebecca, Hannah and Joseph.‡
  Mary, wid., int. 2-17-1740.§

Colson (Coleston), **George,** will 12-3-1721. Wf. Hannah; chd. George, Ann, wf. of William Hutson; Thomas and Hannah. (Last two under age),**

Collson, Thomas, Pilesgrove, will 11-21-1733, pr. 8-8-1750. Bro.

George Collson; sister, Hannah Oakford.‡

Collyer, John. Wf. Elizabeth; chd. Isabel, b 12-22-1690; William, b 11-15-1682; Elizabeth, 9-27-1694; Sarah, 12-20-1696; Percillah, b 12-7-1702; Martha, b 1-9-1704/5; Samuel, b 6-28-1709.†

Condon, John, adm. 3-22-1703/4.‡

Conelly, Brian, m Dorothy Bull, 7-27-1731.¶

Conger, John, Morris River, laborer, inv. 7-27-1726.‡

Congleton, James, int. 2-25-1743/4. Wf. Bridget.‡

Conkelyn, Gideon. Wf. Presulla; chd. Susannah, bap. 4-24-1743; Samuel, bap. 6-21-1746/7.*

Connway, Philipp, Mannington, will 10-11-1713. Wf. Ellce; six chd. not named.**

Conor, John, m Hannah Denn, 1-13-1740/1.*

Cooper, William, came from England and settled at Salem in 1678; blacksmith.††
William. Wf. Mary; chd. Hannah, b 6-7-1686; Mary, b 12-27-1688; Sarah, b 7-15-4691.†
William, Jr., Salem, blacksmith, will 28th of 1st mo. (March), 1691; rec. 12-23-1692. Wf. Mary; chd. John, Hannah and Mary; father-in-law Edward Bradway; father William Cooper.‡

Copner, Cornelius, m Margaret Peterson, 6-15-1732.¶

Cornelious, Stephan, Penns Neck, single man, will 4-4-1726, pr. 7-20-1726. Mother Catrain Staekop.‡ and §

Corneliouson, Cornelious, Middle Neck, inv. 10-27-1702. Bro. Henry Corneliuson.§
Lause, Penns Neck, will 1-22-1701/2, rec. 1-20-1702/3. Wf. Catherine; chd. Eleazar and Christian.§
Michael, Penns Neck, husb., inv. 6-18-1702.§

Cornelius, Lause, Sr., West Fenwick or Castana Neck, planter, will 12-14-1684, pr. 2-14-1686/7. Wf. Britta.‡ and §.

Cornelison, Charles, Penns Neck, will 12-22-1748, pr. 2-23-1750. Wf. Ann; chd. Catherine, Andrew, Charles and John (last three under age.§

Corneliuson, Crnelius, Penns Neck, will 2-25-1743/4, pr. 11-10-1744. Wf. Ann; chd. Jacob, Cornelius, Sarah Tussey, Catherine Butterworth and Elinor Mounson; grandchd. Elinor Butterworth and Peter Boon.‡

Cox, John, weaver, Grinwich, will 3-20-1725/6, pr. 4-11-1726.‡

Craft, William, m Mary Morgan, 4-6-1739.¶

Crafton, Ambrose, petty shopman, Salem Town, int. 11-4-1731.‡

Craig, John. Wf. Mary; chd. Elizabeth, Mary and Martha, all bap. 4-26-1741; James, bap. 6-12-1742; Samuel, bap 3-11-1743/4; Sarah, bap. 12-7-1746; Elias, bap. 10-28-1750.*

Craven, Nehemiah, Cumberland, will 4-22-1749, pr. 5-10-1749. Chd. Thomas and Mary (both under age).‡

Richard, Salem, will 10-27-1748, affirmed 11-15-1748. Wf. Patience; chd. Elizabeth, John, Wheat, Grace and Rachel (all under age).§

Robert. Testimony 31st of 6th mo. (Aug.) 1681. Chd. Thomas, Peeter and Ann. His wid. m Charles Bagley.§

Thomas, farmer, Cohansey, will 9-13-1721, pr. 12-23-1730. Chd. Nehemiah (under age) Elizabeth, Rachel and Anne.**

Crawford, Archibald, cordwainer, Penns Neck, will 11-28-1748, pr. 12-5-1748. Wf. Catteron; chd. John, Mary, Jane and Margaret.‡

Daniel, schoolmaster, int. 3-15-1745/6.‡

Crayne, John, Burlington m Mary Elwell, Salem, 2-19-1727.¶

Crofoot, David, Cohansey, weaver, inv. 7-23-1720.**

Cross, Benjamin, m Virgln Besby, 9-25-1739.¶

Crosthwait, Charles, inv. 1-12-1729/30.**

Crow, George. Eadeth Crow, adm. 4-21-1730.**

Crum, Heyman. Wf. Elizabeth; chd. John, bap. 3-28-1741/2.*

Cullier, Benjamin, husb., Mannington, will 7th of 11th mo. (Jan.), 1748/9, affirmed 3-10-1748/9. Chd. John, Samuel and Rebecca (all under age); cousin Henry Stubbins.‡

Cullyer, John, Mannington Precinct, will 4-29-1728, pr. 5-21-1728. Wf. Elizabeth; chd. William, Benjamin, Samuel, Isbell, Daniel, Priscilla and Martha.**

William, Mannington, husb., will 2-11-1733/4. Chd. Elizabeth, Martha, Isabell and Sarah.‡

Culyer, Samuel, Mannington, will 1-18-1733, affirmed 4-5-1734. Bros. William and Benjamin Cullyer; sister Priscilla Culyer.‡

Curnelius, John, Penns Neck, will 11-13-1691. Chd. Curnelious and Henry who has a dau. Garta, wf. of Marcus Elger.§

Current, Nicholas, m Mary Powel, 9-27-1742.*

Currey, James. Chd. William, bap. 4-4-1742; Robert, bap. 1-5 1745/6; Margaret, bap. 4-1-1750.*

Curryer, Edward, Manneton and Salem Town, will 7-12-1701, rec. 9-26-1701. Wf. Elizabeth; cousins George, John, Joseph and Sarah (all under age), ch.d. of bro.-in-law John Beetle of Philadelphia.§

Curtis, Samuel, Munmouth River, will 1-5-1711/12. Wf. Ann; son-in-law Peter Blackfield; cousins George Beard, George Trenchard, Sr., George Trenchard, Jr., Edward Trenchard and Joan Trenchard.†

Dalbro, Andrew, int. 3-9-1748/9. Catherine Dalbo, adm.‡

Daniel, Aaron. Wf. Rebecca; chd David, b 3-4-1749.†

Daniel, Stowe Creek, will 12-20-1694, signed Daniel Daniel, but called Daniel Denn in will, inventory and probate. Wf. Elizabeth.—
East Jersey Wills, Liber A.

James. Wf. Jane; chd. Jane, b 10-2-1701; Thomas, b 1-2-1703; James, b 8-12-2704; Isabel, b 3-2-1706; Mary, b 8-20-1707; Joseph, b 3-3-1709; Sarah, b 3-3-1709 †

James. Wf. Isabel; chd. Elizabeth, b 12-19-1714; Rebeckah, b 9-6-1716; John, b 8-25-1718; William, b 1-26-1721; Aaron, b 6-21-1723.

John, Cohansie, will 4-26-1735, pr. 5-2-1735.‡

William. Wf. Rebecca; chd. James, b 3-17-1743; Joseph, b 1-14-1745; Thomas, b 6-23-1747; Sarah, b 11-2-1749; William, b 7-25-1755; Jael, b 10-10-1759; Edmund, b 1-14-1762; John, b 12-4-1657.†

Daniell, Elizabeth, wid., Salem, will 6th of 2d mo. (April), 1684, pr. 7-22-1684. Chd. William, Richard and Elizabeth Waithman.—
Monmouth Wills.

James, Stow Creek, will 12-19-1726, pr. 1-11-1726/7 Wf. Isabell; chd. Thomas, James, Joseph, John, William, Aron, Jane Butcher, Isabell, Sarah, Elizabeth and Rebeckah.‡

William, Greenwich, will 3-14-1706/7, pr. 4-25-1707. Wf. Ellenor; sister Elizabeth, wf. of William Waithman; cousins William, James, John, Thomas and Elizabeth Waithman.‡

Daniels James, Alloways Creek, m Elizabeth Barber, Elsenborough, 7-29-1736.†

William, ward, 16 years, 10-28-1737.‡

Danielson, Jacobus, int. 4-3-1734. Mary Danielson, adm.‡

Darbyshire, John, cooper, int. 11-9-1734.§

Dare, William, Cohansey, will 2-1-1747/8, pr. 12-6-1749. Wf. Elizabeth; chd. William, John, Mary Jessup, Hannah Ogden, Elizabeth Preston, Rachel Westcott and Sarah Westcott.‡

Dark, Samuel, fuller, Grinwich, Cohansey Precinct, will 12-30-1728, pr. 8-12-1729. Wf. Ruth; dau. Ruth (under age); dau.-in-law (?step-daugh.) Margaret Johns (alias Pope), wf. of Thomas Johns of Kent, Del.‡

Darkin, Ann, wid., Windham, will 1st of 3d mo., 1717, pr. 12-30-1718. Chd Joseph, John, Hannah Hosier, Ann (under age); grandchd. Joseph Whitten.‡

Hannah, dau. Joseph Darkin late of Elsinborough, ward, 11-11-1738. Stepmother Hannah Darkin; cousin, Sarah Wyat.‡

John, s of Richard, m Sarah. dau of Thomas and Jale Thompson. Chd. Jale, b 11-10-1718, m John, s of Abel Nicholson; John, b 1720, left no issue.∥

John. Wf. Sarah; chd. Jale, b 10-11-1718.†

Joseph, s of Richard, m 1719, Ann, dau. of Isaac Smart Chd. Hannah, b 18th of 10th mo., 1722.∥

Joseph. Wf. Ann; chd. Hannah, b 10-13-1722; Sarah, b 2-11-1726.†

Joseph, int. 4-14-1739. Wf. Hannah; dau. Hannah.‡

Richard. Wf. Ann; chd. Joseph, b 1-3-1688 at Windham, near Salem; Hannah, b 9-3-1691; John, b 5-9-1694; Ann, b 1-31-1700.†

Richard, Windham, will 1-6-1707/8, pr. 4-26-1716. Wf. Ann; chd. Sarah, wf. of James Whitton; Joseph, John, Hannah and Ann (last four under age).**

Daten, Ephraim, Jr., Fairfield Twp., int. 1-21-1750/1. Father Ephraim Daten.‡

Jacob, int 9-4-1742. Wf. Ann.‡

Dauson (Dawson), **William,** Alloways Creek, int. 1-20-1749/50. Wf. Margaret.‡

Davies, Arthur, m Hester Preston of Deerfield, 12-6-1743. Chd. Luri, bap. 8-17-1746.*

Benjamin, m Ann Foster, 8-13-1748.*

Daniel, Deerfield. Wf. Anna; chd. Broadway, Amon, Uriah, Joseph, all bap. before 4-15-1744; Arthur, bap. 1-26-1745/6; Hannah, bap. 10-30-1748.*

James. Wf. Mary; Chd. Abishai, Sarah, Othniel, Rachel, all bap. 5-6-1743; Joanna, bap. 5-6-1744; Elizabeth, bap. 4-27-1746; Hester, bap. 10-30-1748.*

Davis, Arthur, Deerfield. Wf. Martha; chd. Daniel, bap. 3-27-1742/3.*

Benjamin, int. 2-27-1732. Esther Davis and Benjamin Davis, adm.‡

Benjamin, int. 12-17-1736.‡

Charles, Cohansey, m Rachel Dennis, Elsenboro, 9-7-1739.†

Charles. Wf. Rachel; chd. Gabriel, b. 5-22-1743.†

Elias, int. 5-12-1736.‡

Gabril, Cohansie, will 4-1-1711. Wf. Jane; chd. Charles and Elias (both under age).‡

Isaac, Pilesgrove, will 3-25-1739, affirmed 6-1-1739. Wf. Elizabeth; chd. Eleanor Crawley, who has a s William; Rachel Morgan, who has sons Isaac and Samuel; Abigail Bassett and Hannah Nelson.‡

John, with sons John, Isaac, Malachi and David, came from Long Island.††

John. Wf. Elenor; chd Mary, b 4-24-1713; Phebe b 2-3-1716; Charity, b 1-3-1717/18; Thomas, 11-13-1719; Hannah, b 2-15-1721; Elizabeth, b 1-9-1723; Marv, b 8-10-1726; John, b 5-13-1730.†

John, Pilesgrove Twp., will 3d of 7th mo. (September), 1734, affirmed 5-16-1735. Chd. Thomas, John, Mary, Phebe and Charity; bros. David and Malichi Davis.‡

John, Pilesgrove, will 10-12-1737, affirmed 5-16-1737. Wf. Ann.‡

Malachi, will 5-23-1731, affirmed 4-21-1735. Wf. Rebecca; chd. John, (under age); bros. John and David Davis and John Brick.‡

Dayton, Abraham, Salem, will 3-20-1744, affirmed 4-26-1745.‡

Ephraim, Cohansie, m Buhanna Elmer, Cohansie, 12-29-1747.¶

Ephraim m Sarah Ogden, 5-9 or 5-29- 1747.¶

Peter, Cohansey, will 11-3-1744, pr. 12-8-1744. Wf. Hannah; dau. Lusey; cousin David Dayton.‡

Samuel (Daton, Daynton), Greenage. Wf. Dorothy; chd. Peter, Samuel and Luce (all under age).‡

Deacon, George, s of George. b at Church Waltham, County Essex, felt maker and citizen of London, in the 36th year of his age, with wf. Frances, born at Difford, in County Kent, his father, and Thomas Edwards his manservant, came to West Jersey in the Willing Mind, arriving at Salem 10-3-1677; removed to Alloways Creek.†

Deane, Andrew, schoolmaster, Salem, int. 10-15-1739.‡

Joseph, Cohansey, will 11-19-1716, pr. 1-25-1716/17. Wf. Mary; chd. Joseph (under age), Hannah and Mary.‡

Dear, Benoni, m Kesire Stedman, 11-8-1745.¶

Demsey, Timothy, Penns Neck, will 9-11-1733, pr. 9-23-1733. Wf. Ann; s John (under age).‡

Denn, James, m in 1688, Elizabeth, dau. of James Maddox. Chd. Margaret, b 29th of 4th mo., 1689; John, b 11th of 6th mo., 1693, m in 1717, Elizabeth, dau of Charles and Mary Oakford.‖

James, Munmouth River, turner, will 17th of 8th mo. (October),

1693, rec. 2-26-1693/4. Wf. Elizabeth; Chd. John and dau. not named (both under age); bro. Daniel Denn; sister Mary Denn.§

John, "d at or before ye 24th day of June, 1685." Letters test. granted 11-8-1686. Wf. Margrett.§

John. Wf. Elizabeth; chd. Elizabeth, b 12-13-1713; James, b 1-8-1716/17; Naomy, b 1-19-1718/19; John, b 7-25-1721.†

John. Wf. Lea; chd. Marcy, b 1-21-1724; Amos, b 7-21-1727; Daniel, b 8-1-1728; Leah, b 8-18-1734; Paul, b 2-18-1734.†

John, int. 12-18-1733. Wf. Lea.**

John. Wf. Elizabeth; chd. Rachel, b 2-30-1745; James, b 11-19-1746/7; John, b 3-5-1751; David, b 7-3-1756.†

John, Alloways Creek, m Elizabeth Bacon, Cohansey, 9-15-1743.†

John, s of John Maddox Denn, m Elizabeth, dau. of John and Elizabeth (Smith) Bacon. Chd. Elizabeth, m William s of Andrew Griscom; James, John, David, Martha, b 1758.‖

Leah, Alloways Creek, int. 2-2-1749.‡

Denis (Dennis), **Jonathan, Jr.,** Cohansey, weaver, will 7-27-1715, pr. 8-16-1715. Wf. Sarah; chd. Rachel and Sarah.‡

Dennes, Jonathan, Cohansey,, will 8-9-1719, pr. 5-31-1720. Wf. Rachel; chd. Phillep, Charles and Samuel.‡

Dennis (Denix), **John,** Cohansey, will 5-4-1715, pr. 10-4-1727. Wf. Hannah; chd. Henry (under age), Hannah, Rachel and Sarah.‡ and *Gloucester Wills.*

Philip. Wf. Lucy; chd. Martha, b 7-15-1724; Prudence, b 9-19-1726; Philip, b 11-19-1731; Grace, b 7-7-1740; Rachel, b 4-6-1742, Elizabeth, b 5-29-1747; Jonathan, b 6-4-1750.†

Samuel. Wf. Ann; chd. John, b 10-15-1718; Elizabeth, b 3-20-1724; Ann, b 3-10-1729; Dorcas, b 12-6-1730/31; Samuel, b 5-29-1747; Sarah, b 12-8-1733/4.†

Samuel, int. 3-31-1735. Wf. Anne.‡

Derwin, Ebenezer, int. 4-10-1733. Elizabeth Derwin, Adm.‡

Derewitt, Benjamin, inv. 4-7-1709.**

Deul, John. Wf. Hannah; chd. John, b 3-25-1732.†

Deurox, Alexander, husb., will 5-24-1711, pr. 7-25-1711. Chd. Rachel and Rebecka (both under age).

Devos, Mathias, m Elizabeth Johnson, 10-16-1740.¶

Dewildy, John, inv. 1-1-1706/7.**

Dibble, Thomas, int. 12-17-1744.‡

Dickason, Jonathan, husb., will 2-11-1748/9, affirmed 3-10-1748. Wf. Dorothy; chd. John and Nathaniel.‡

William, Salem, m Abigail Ward, Gloucester, 11-21-1749.¶

Dickinson, Fenwick, Pilesgrove, will 6-21-1739, pr. 12-19-1739. Wf. Eleanor, who m Thomas Murphy; chd. John, Joseph (under age), Susannah, Abraham, Isaac, Isabell, Eleanor (last four under age), and Sarah. Ages in 1739: Eleanor 5, Elizabeth 8, Isaac 6, Abraham 4, Joseph 2.‡

John, Salem, m Lydomia Belton, Gloucester, 10-27-1747.¶

Dickson, Anthony, Greenwich, will 2-13-1700/1, rec. 6-4-1701. Wf. Elizabeth; chd. James, Martha, Daniel and Anthony.§

Dillon, James, m Mary Dillon, 9-20-1739.¶

Ditty, Hugh, Penns Neck, will 12-5-1748, pr. 12-13-1748. Wf. Hannah; chd. John, Thomas, Martha, Margret.‡

Dixon, Anthony, Cohansey, inv. 12-23-1728. Mary Dixon, adm.**
Anthony, m Elizabeth Camell, 1-8-1683/4.¶

Daniel, ward, s of Anthony and Mary Dixon, south side of Cohansey, 5-29-1740.§

James, Greenwich, Cohansey, 1-2-1738, pr. 1-15-1739. Wf. Rebecca; chd. Sarah, Rachel, Isabel.‡

Donne, Robert, Alloways Creek, will 10-16-1694; rec. 12-3-1694. Cousins James Budd, Philadelphia, and Samuel Curtice.§

Doubleday, William, int. 12-16-1740.**

Draper, Edward. Wf. Mary; chd. Thomas, b 9-21-1747; Jael, b 8-25-1749; Rebeckah, b 9-8-1751; Mary, b 2-16-1754; Amy, b 6-10-1756; Jemima, b 10-27-1758.†

Driver, Jonathan, shoemaker, Penns Neck, int., 4-10-1749. Elizabeth Driver, adm.‡

DuBois, Barent, Pilesgrove, will 12-22-1749, pr. 2-20-1749/50. Wf. Jacomyntie; chd. Jacob, Jonathan, Katherine Elwell, Solomon, David, Isaac, Gerret and Abraham.‡

Garrett. Wf. Margaret; dau. Sarah, bap. 7-4-1742.*

Jacob. Chd. Barnett, Catharine, b 1716; Jacob, b 1719, m Janette Newkirk in 1747; Louis, b 1695, m Margaret Jansen in 1720.††

Jacob, Sr., m Janite Nieukirk, 6-3-1747. Dau. Rachel, bap. 10-29-1749.*

Lewis. Wf. Margaret; s Samuel, bap. 3-7-1741/2.*

Duffel, William. Wf. Catharine; s Jacob, bap. 3-11-1749/50.‡

Dugdall, Thomas, tailor, Mannington, will 10-13-1713, pr, 6-9-1714.‡

Duncan, Elizabeth, int. 8-21-1749.**
James, Alloways Creek, int. 7-13-1748. Elizabeth Duncan, adm.‡
John, weaver, int. 1-9-1748.‡

Dunlap, Francis. Wf. Isabel; chd. Thomas, bap. 12-26-1742; Aaron, bap. 2-17-1944; Francis and John, both bap. 4-30-1741 Aarnn, bap. 2-17-1744; Ḟrancis, bap. 9-6-1747.*
Francis, m Elizabeth Hunter, 5-18-1744.*
Francis. Wf. Rebeckah; dau. Rebeckah, bap. 5-23-1748.*
Francis, Pilesgrove Twp., will 5-19-1748, pr. 5-15-1749. Wf. Rebecca; chd. Mary and Bathsheba.‡
James, m Elizabeth Worthington, 3-29-1731.¶
James, m Ann Hunter, 1-24-1746.¶
James. Wf. Ann; chd. Bathsheba, bap. 3-13-1747/8; Mary, bap. 4-16-1749.*

Dunn, Jeremiah, Piscataway, m Margaret Carman, Salem, 5-14-1747.¶
Dunn, John, m Elizabeth Wheaton, 1-18-1733.¶
John, Penns Neck, int., 12-6-1742. Wf. Sarah.‡
Zacheus, b 12-2-1698/9. Wf. Deborah, b 2 10-1708; chd. Naomi, b 11-6-1728/9; Sarah, b 11-30-1730/31; John, b 10-26-1732, d 6th mo., 1745; Mary, b 9-22-1735, d 6th mo., 1745; Isaac, b 12-2-1737/8, d 6th mo.,1745; Nathan, b 12-25-1742/3, d 2-19-1782; Deborah, b 4-6-1745; John, b 10-25-1747, d 11-6-1747.†

Dyer, John, m Elinor Short, 3-26-1730.¶
John, doctor, Greenwich, will 1-11-1732/3, pr. 11-24-1732.‡

Eastland(Estland), **Joseph,** Cohanzy, will 12-9-1728, pr. 12-24-1728. Wf. Ann; grandson-in-law Mark Reeve (under age).**
William, Cohansie, will 8-28-1713, pr. 2-22-1714/15. Wf. Sarah; chd. Thomas and Joseph; bros. Joseph and John Eastland.‡

Eaton, Benjamin, Sr., will 10-4-1734, pr. 12-7-1734. Wf. Margaret; chd. Benjamin, Sarah and Ann.‡
John, husb., Penns Neck; will 4-21-1748, pr. 4-30-1748. Wf. Sarah; chd. John, Henry and Elizabeth.‡
Michael, came as a servant of John Fenwick, 1675 ††
Simon, husb., Penns Neck, inv. 7-25-1727. Madlen Eaten of Penns Neck, adm.**

Ebrecht, John, m Elizabeth Hogbin, 11-14-1749.*

Eglington, Edward, inv., 4-30-1729. Jeane Eglington, adm.‡

Elegar (Eldgar, Elgar, **Marcus,** bachelor, Middle Neck, will 1-1-1703/4, pr. 1-18-1708/9. Mother Gartheret Jones; nephews Thomas Buckley and John Winton; aunts Rachel Jones and Hannah Elegar.‡

Elger, Marcus, will 11-2-1694, rec. 1-9-1694/5. Wf. Gertrude; chd. Marcus, John, Mary, Rachel, Hannah.§

Elwell, Hannah, spinster, Penns Neck, bond of adm. 10-28-1728.**

Jacob, emigrant, b in England in 1700, m Catharine DuBois. Chd. David, Samuel, Jonathan, Rhoda, m 1st, Henry Richmond, 2d, William Ray, 3d, Josiah Paullin; Rachel, m James Hutchinson.‖

John, int. 6-11-1737.

Samuel, Pilesgrove Twp., will 1-5-1739/40, affirmed 2-16-1739. Wf. Famzen; chd. Jacob, Samuel, Abraham, Rachel, m William Brick; Susanna, m John Ray; Elizabeth, Famzen, Coziah, Phebe, Molley and Tobitha.‡

Samuel m Susanna Elwell, 11-25-1745.*

Thomas, Pilesgrove precinct, will 8-14-1722, pr. 2-17-1724. Wf. Susannah; chd; Thomas and Josiah.**

Elwill, William, will 21st of 11th mo., 1728/9, pr. 2-17-1728/9. Wf. Ann; chd. John, William, Sarah and Hannah; brother Samuel Elwill.**

Encloes (Enlows, Inloes), **Peter,** Penns Neck, will 11-11-1743, pr. 11-23-1743. Chd. Peter, Joseph, Anthony, Ales Giljohnson, Elizabeth Philpot.‡

Eratt (Erratt), **Francis,** joiner, Mannington precinct, will 2-19-1927/8, pr. 3-8-1727/8.**

Erickson, John, husb., Lucas Point, will pr. 6-17-1691. Wf. Maggdelena; chd. Bridgett, Barbara, Katherine and Annake; son-in-law John Stalcup.§

Errickson, Andrew, Sr., mariner, Morrisses River, will 1-31-1747, pr.5-24-1748. Wf. Modlena; chd. Andrew, Samuel, Christiana Peterson, Sarah Huings, and Rebecca.‡

Erriott (Errit), **Joseph,** laborer, bond of adm. 2-26-1728/9.**

Estland, Ann, Cohansey, wid., will 11-4-1730, pr. 4-26-1735. Grandchd. Mark, Joseph, John and Martha Reeves (all under age).‡

Euaens (Evance, Evans), **James,** tailor, Alloways Creek, inv. 1-17-1728/9. Mary Evance, adm.‡

Evans, David, clerk, Pilesgrove,, will 7-25-1749, pr. 3-9-1750. Wf. Ann, chd. Samuel, who has chd. Hannah, Israel and Ann.‡

Nathaniel, int. 10-22-1750.§
John, shallopman, int. 1-2-1747‡
Sarah, b 1-19-1745/6.†

Ewing, Thomas, Scotch-Irish emig. came from Londonderry to Long Island in 1718, and soon to Greenwich. Eldest s, Maskell.††

Thomas, Sr., Cohansey, will 1-7-1744/5, pr. 4-7-1748. Wf. Mary; chd. John, Thomas, Mary, Samuel, Joshua and James.‡

William, husb., Cohansey, will 4-7-1749, pr. 5-1-1749. Bro. James Ewing.‡

Ewen, John, m Mary Pledger, 8-21-1745.¶

Ezard (Ezzard, Issard, Izard), **Mickael,** Prince Morrisses River, inv. 9-13-1722. Wf. Martha.‡

Fairbanks, Edward, cordwainer, Cohanzey, inv., 2-20-1727/8.**

Robert, b in Lestershire, Eng., abt. 1632, re. to Ireland abt. 1653, and in 1676 m Sarah, b at Spenceford, Somersetshire, dau of Thomas Leonard. Wtih wf. and dau. Elizabeth Stubings (dau. by a former marriage), and Henry Stubings, her husband, came to West Jersey in the "Mary of Dublin," landing at Elsinburg, 12-22-1677.†

Fairebanck, Robert, tailor, Elsenburgh, inv. 9-23-1678. Wf. Sarah, who m John Thompson, carpenter, of Elsenburgh, before 11-13-1682.§

Farr, Henry, int., 11-25-1745. Hannah Farr, adm ‡

Fenwick, John, late of Benfield, county Berks, Eng., now of Fenwick's Colony, will 8-7-1683, pr. 4-16-1784. Grandchd. Fenwick Adams, Samuel Hedge, Jr., John Champneys, Mary Champneys, Walter Adams, Mary Adams, Ann Adams; bro. Capt. Ralfe Fenwick who has a s Roger; dau. Ann, wf. of Samuel Hedge of Hedgefield; Elizabeth Adams, prob. a granddau.§

Fetters, Mary, Salem. Adm. granted 1-24-1721/2.‡

Thomas, Salem, int. 12-23-1732.‡

Field, Mary, wid., Grinwich, will 4-2-1726, pr. 4-11-1726.‡

Thomas, husb., Mannington precinct, will 4-3-1723, pr- 4.16-1726. Wf. Mary; son-in-law Zachariah Barrar; "my" child Sollaman Winsor (under age).‡

Firth, John, Alloways Creek, will 3-16-1718/19, pr. 12-8-1719. Wf. Sarah; s John (under age); father Edward Firth; bro. Edward Firth.‡ *and Gloucester Wills.*

John. Wf. Judith; chd. Ezra, b 1-24-1744/5; Sarah, b 9-13-1747;

Elizabeth, b 5-2-1751, O.S.; John, b 8-26-1754 (another entry says 9-5-1754); Henry, b 8-19-1756.†

John. Wf. Sarah; chd. Edward, b 9-3-1710; John, b 7-3-1718.†

Fisher, Dennis, shipwright, of Portsmouth, Eng., now of Alloways Creek, will 2-14-1690/1, rec. 10-30 1690/1. Wf. Susannah; sisters Susan Young and Elizabeth Simmons.§

Susanna, wid., will 11-18-1707, pr. 4-1-1708. Chd. Henry, Elisabeth, and John; grandchd. Susanna, Sarah, Henry and Elisabeth Fisher.‡

Fitchrandolph, Christopher, Cohansy. Bond of adm. 12-30-1715.‡

Peter, Cohansey. Bond of adm. 4-22-1730.**

Fithian, John, husb., Fairfield. Adm. granted 3-9-1702/3. Mother Priscilla Fithian.§

Jonathan, Esq., Cohansey, will 8-3-1737, pr. 4-29-1743. Wf. Sarah; chd. Jonathan, David, Phebe, wf. of William Stratton, and Sarah, wf. of Thomas Baitman.‡

Jonathan, int. 12-3-1742. Jonathan Fithian, Jr., eldest son, Cohansey, farmer.‡

Josiah, s of Samuel and Priscilla (dau. of Thomas and Mary Bennett of Southampton, L. I.), b 5-6-1865, m Sarah, dau. of Philip Dennis, minister of the Friends' Society. Chd. Samuel, b 10-12-1715, m 9-3-1741, Phebe, dau. of Ephraim Seeley of Bridgeton. He was Sheriff 1750, Justice, Judge, Rep. to Provincial Congress 1775. He d 11-2-1777. His wf d 3-12-1764.††

Josiah, m Mary Johnson, 6-2-1733.¶

Josiah, Esq , Cohansey, will 3-31-1741, pr. 4-24-1741. Wf. Mary; chd. Mary, Jeremiah, Samuel, Joseph, Hannah Seeley..‡

Matthias, carpenter, Cumb. Co., will 5-29-1749, pr. 10-24-1749. Chd. Humphrey, Daniel, deceased; William, Ephraim and 6 others.‡

Samuel, Fairfield, will 7-3-1702, rec. 3-1-1702/3. Wf. Priscilla; chd. John, Josiah, Samuel, Easter, Mathias, William and Isaac.§

Samuel, s of Samuel and Priscilla, settled in Greenwich abt. 1705.††

William, carpenter, Greenwich, will 1-27-1732, pr. 2-16-1732. Bros. Samuel and Mathias Fithian.‡

Fitzgerald (Fitzgarill), **Edward,** carpenter, Cohansey, int. 1-25-1734/5.‡

Fitzrandolph, David, m Jael Darkin, 5-25-1740.¶

Flanegan, Thomas, m Elizabeth Smith, 12-1-1739.¶

Fleetwood, William, laborer, Alloways Creek, inv. 3-18-1717/18.‡

Fling, George, m Margaret Dickey, 1-22-1735.¶

Fogg, Charles, m Hannah Miller (both of Greenwich), 7-2-1746. Chd. Hannah, b 11-10-1749/50.‡

Joseph, Cohansey, will 1-30-1705/6, pr. 3-8-1705/6. Wf. Sarah.‡

Joseph. Wf. Elizabeth; chd. David, b 10-30-1738; Ebenezer, b 3-26-1741; Charles; b 2-29-1743; Hannah, b 12-5-1744/5; Ann, b 3-23-1747, d 7-17-1751; Elizabeth, b 11-1-1749/50, Holme, b 3-28-1752; Isaac, b 3-17-1755; Rebeckah, b 5-22-1758; Mary, d January 1759.†

Samuel, inv. 1-16-1709/10.‡

Folwell, William, Salem, inv. 10-13-1710. Wf. Hope.‡

Footit, John, schoolmaster, Elsenburgh, will 30th of 11th mo. (Jan.), 1719/20.‡

Foredam (Fordam), **Charles,** cordwainer. Greenwich, int. 5-5-1740. Wf. Elizabeth.‡

Forrest, John, m Ann Davies, 2-17-1740/1. Chd. Barbara, bap-12-19-1741.*

Foster (Forster), **David,** North Side of Cohansey, will 3-9-1727/8, pr. 5-29-1728. Wf. Joanna; dau. Mary Sayer.‡

Jeremiah. Wf. Patient; chd. Abigail, bap. 6-13-1742.*

Thomas, Penns Neck, will 4-2-1705, pr. 3-20-1706-7. Wf. Elizabeth.**

William, farmer, Mannington, will 11-28-1747, pr. 12-12-1747 Wf. Ann; chd. Mary, Rebecca and Elizabeth.‡

Franson, Ann, wid., Penns Neck, bond of adm. 1-2-1718/9.‡

Philip, Penns Neck, will 2-26-1726/7, pr. 2-21-1726/7. Wf. Elener.**

Freeman, John, Cohansey, will 1-10-1715/16. Bond of adm. 7-18-1719. Wf. Mary; chd. Anthony.**

French, Thomas, m Isabel Mason, 7-13-1733.¶

Friend, Charles, Penns Neck, will 4-17-1749, affirmed 4-26-1749. Cousins Andrew and Isaac Friend (both under age).‡

Ephraim m Bridgitta Snecks, 6-5-1731.‡

Johannes, husb., Penns Neck, will 3-8-1737, pr. 2-1-1737/8. Chd. Andrew, Charles, Neals, Ephraim, John, Nanne, Mary and Sary, who has a dau.‡

Fritch, Phillip, int. 9-1-1743.§

Fry, John, m Mary Braithwaite, 5-4-1727.¶

John, mariner, inv. 8-11-1729. Mary Fry, adm.‡

Fuller, John, m Ellenor Lewis, 7-16-1683.¶

John, planter, Cesariae River, Cohansey, will 10-23-1695, rec. 12-10-1695.§

Fullerton, James, merchant, Fairfield, Cohansey, inv. 1-22-1729/30.‡

Furbush, Thomas, carpenter, Fairfield, inv. 4-20-1702.§

Gabaits (Gabadis), **Rebeckah,** Allowayes Creek, will 3-24-1725/6, pr. 5-30-1726.‡]

Gandouett, Francis, Salem Town, will 3-11-1733, pr. 3-29-1733. Wf. Anna; s Francis (under age); father-in-law Samuel Smith.‡

Gandy, John, Morris River, int. 6-27-1748. Wf. Susanna.‡
Samuel, Morris River, int. 6-27-1748. Hannah Gandy, wid., Gloucester Co., adm.‡
Thomas, Cumberland Co., will 5-21-1748, pr. 9-5-1748. Chd. Aaron, David, Patience, Catherine, Sarah, Mary, Phebe, Hannah, Priscilla, Rebecca, Naomy; son-in-law Nathan Shaw.‡

Garral, Rebecca, Alloways Creek, will 9-26-1750, pr. 12-8-1750. Chd. John, Mary, Hannah and Susanah.‡

Garrison, Arthur. Wf. Sarah; chd. John, Sarah, Jane and Daniel, all bap. 8-17-1740.*
Benjamin. Wf. Tamson; chd. Miriam, bap. 4-14-1743; Rachel, bap. 5-22-1743; Phebe, bap. 9-23-1744; Jonathan, bap. 10-12-1746; Abigail, bap. 3-19-1748/9.*
David. Wf. Mary; chd. John, bap. 8-10-1740; Joseph, bap. 2-5-1742/3.*
Frederick, Pilesgrove, inv. 1-9-1728/9. Elizabeth Garrison, adm.**
Frederick, Jr., Salem, int. 4-12-1749.‡
Isaac, m Elizabeth Lawrence, 3-24-1727.¶
Isaac, m Hannah Bennett, 12-30-1740; chd. Isaac, bap. 4-14-1743; Mary, bap. 10-9-1743; Hannah, bap. 9-7-1746.*
Jacob, Cohanzy, will 9-4-1705, pr. 9-19-1709. Wf. Christiana; chd. Abraham and Isaac; grandson Isaac, s of Isaac and Lidian Garrison ‡
Jeremiah. Wf. Mary; chd. Gamaliel, bap. 8-10-1740; Abigail, bap. 10-11-1741; Joel, bap 1-30-1742/3; Abigail, bap. 2-24-1745; Phebe, bap. 1-25-1746/7; John, bap. 7-31-1748; Hannah, bap. 5-20-1750.*
John. Wf. Amey; dau. Hannah, bap 6 6-1742.*
John T., int. 3-10-1747. Elizabeth Garrison, adm.‡
Joshua. Wf. Sarah; chd. Elizabeth, bap. 4-4-1741/2; David, bap. 4-6-1746.*
Seger, m Susanna Huckings, 5-30-1738.¶

Garritt. George, will 13th of 7th mo. (Sept.), 1714. pr. 9-28-1715. Wf. Elizabeth; chd. George and Bartholamu.‡

Gibbon, Leonard, will 6-4-1744, affirmed 7-4-1744. Chd. Leonard John (under age); bro. Nicholas Gibbon.‡

Nicholas, m Anne Hedge, 3-16-1731.

Gibson, Joseph. Wf. Elizabeth; chd. Rachel, b 7-3-1721; Sarah, b 12-2-1722/3; Elizabeth, b 8-7-1724, Joseph, b 3-28-1726.†

Gilham, Constant, wid., Salem Town, will pr. 3-31-1708. Chd Elizabeth Gambell, Elizabeth Gilham and Avis Gilham.‡

Robert, carpenter, Salem Town, will 2-17-1705/6. Wf. Constant; chd. William and Lucas (both under 20), Elizabeth, Evis and Ann (all under 18) ‡

Gillaspie, John, m Elizbbeth Lord, 10-19-1749.*

Gilchrist, Thomas, int. 2-16-1750. Daniel Murfy and Margaret Murphy, late Gilchrist, adms.‡

Gillett, Joshua, Penns Neck. will 12-15-1691, rec. 8-10-1692. Wf˙ Margrett; chd. Thomas and others not named.§

Gilpin, Thomas, husb,, Penns Neck, inv. 8-10-1697. Wf. Alice.§

Gilljohnson, Elizabeth, wid. of Rennere van Hyst, and wf. of William Gilljohnson.§

Giles. int. 1-21-1733.‡

John, Penns Neck, will 7-23-1721, pr. 8-2-1721. Son William (under age); bro. Thomas.‡

Thomas, s of William, d 1721. Wf. Eleanor (she m abt. 1723, Thomas Miles); chd. Christiana, Rhina, wf. of Erick Gilljohnson; Alice, Sarah, wf. of Andrew s of Sinnick Sinnickson; Catherine and Rebecca.‖

William, will 3-29-1708, pr. 5-29-1709. Chd. Thomas and John; son-in-law (?stepson) Eric Johnson; granddau. Rina Giljohnson.§

Gilman, Edward, Cohansey, will 10-13-1715, pr. 5-7-1716. Wf. Hannah; chd. Edward, Abraham, David, Elizabeth, Martha and Sarah; bro. John Bacon.**

Owen, m Elinor Barber, 1-18-1731.¶

Gillman, John, Pilesgrove, int 1-27-1731.‡

John, Sr., Cesariae River, will 10-14-1685, rec. 12-9-1695. Wf. Rachel; chd Edward, Mercye, Mary, Rachel, Charles, Elizabeth, and Sarah Hutchings.§

Rachel, wid. of John, inv. 3-20-1695/6. Son-in-law (?stepson) Edward Gillman.§

Glann (Glenn), **Katrene,** Morrises River, will 4-15-1727, pr. 6-10-1728. Chd. Lazarus and Zacharias who has daus. Mary and Katrene ‡

Godwin, Edward, Penns Neck. will 5-26-1707, pr. 2-10-1708. First wf., Mary, buried at John Thompson's; second wf. Frances; bro. and sister in Ireland, Thomas and Elizabeth Godwin; bros. Larance Daues and George Stacy.‡

Goodwin, John, laborer, Manington, inv. 1-9-1726/7.**

John, s of John and Katherine, of Parish Buttolph Aldgate, Houndsditch, London, b 10-25-1680; re. to Pennsylvania, 1701, and from thence to Salem; m Susannah, dau. of John Smith of Hedgefield, formerly of Krindail Parish, Kent.†

John, bricklayer, Salem, will 25th of 3d mo. (May), 1731, pr. 5-16-1733. Wf. Susanna; chd. Mary Jones, Joseph, John, Thomas and William (sons under age).‡

John. Wf. Susannah; chd. John, b 12-29-1707; Richard, b 7-4-1709; Mary, 9-1-1710; Joseph, b 11-21-1713; John, b 10-17-1716; Thomas, b 6-10-1721; William, b 8-25-1723.†

Joseph, int. 7-10-1742. Wf. Sarah.‡

Joseph. Wf. Sarah; chd. Richard, b 7-29-1739; Pheby, b 5-8-1741; Joseph, b 10-8-1742.†

Thomas, s of John and Susan Goodwin, m first, Sarah, dau. of Lewis Morris of Elsinborough; she d 1765, leaving no issue. He m second, Sarah Smith, who d 1783. He d 1803.‖

William, s of John and Susannah, b 1723, m 1744, Mary, dau. of Lewis Morris. Chd. John, b 1745; Lewis, Susannah, Mary and William.‖

Gould, Alexander, Stowe Creek, weaver, inv. 5-3-1697. Mother Jane Gould, wid.

Graham, William, laborer, int. 12-21-1741. Cousin William Graham, Pilesgrove.‡

William, alias Grimes. Wf. Judith; s Richard, bap. 5-14-1749. (See Grimes).*

Grant, Alexander, will 1-20-1726/7, pr. 2-21-1726/7. Wf. Ann; chd. Ann Hedge and Barbara.‡

Graves, Thomas, will 9-12-1714, pr. Dec. 20 or 28, 1714. Wf. Anne; chd. Thomas, Joseph and Samuel (all under age); bro.-in-law Aquilla Barber.†

Thomas. Wf. Rebecca; s Thomas, b 8th mo. 1742.†

Green, Daniel, int. 1-5-1735. Wf. Anne.‡

John, blacksmith, Cohansey, will 9-18-1696, rec. 11-4-1696. Wf. Ursula; chd. Timothy, Elizabeth and Lydia.§

Greenman, William, m Elizabeth Vanmeter, 4-24-1730.¶

Gregg, Ann, (former wf. of Richard Woodnut) wid. of William Gregg of Christiana Hundred, Newcastle Co., Del., will 4-20-1747, affirmed 5-7-1747. Chd. Jonathan and Henry Woodnut and Abraham Gregg; sister Rachel, wf. of Jonathan Womsley.‡

Gregory, Joseph, Salem, m Elizabeth Bonell, Philadelphia, 1-6-1727.¶

Joseph, Salem, will 6-9-1740, inv. 6-10-1740. Dau. Elizabeth, wf. of William Barker.‡

Renier, m Hannah Wade, 2-10-1731.¶

Greismeyer, Simeon, int. 5-23-1748.‡

Grimes, Archibald, m Margaret McGoogan, 12-4-1744.*
George, Salem, m Mary Rodgers, Burlington; 8-29-1743.¶
Joseph, will 6-4-1705, pr. 3-18-1705/6. Wf. Mary; s Joseph.‡
William (see Graham). Wf. Judith; chd. Elizabeth, bap. 11-24-1743; Mary, bap. 2-2-1745/6.*

Griscom, Andrew, emig. from England in 1680. Wf Sarah Dole; chd. Tobias, m Deborah Gabitas; Sarah.‖

Grisse, John, Oaldmans Creek, inv. 1st of 6th mo. (Aug.) 1688. Wf. Ann.§

Grist, Jonathan, Penns Neck, int. 2-1-1748. Elizabeth Grist, adm.‡

Guy, Richard, cheesemonger in England. Wf. Bridget.††

Haas, Peter. Son Abraham, bap. 7-26-1741.*

Hackett, David, int. 4-3-1742, Wf. Elizabeth.‡
Thomas, int. 7-27 1733.‡
William, int. 2-23-1737.‡

Hains, Richard. Wf. Agnes; chd. Joseph, b 7-23-1722; Anthony, b 1st mo., 1726; Ephraim, b 7-23-1733; Richard, b 5-3-17—; Rebeckah, b 1-4-1734.†

Haines, Thomas, husb., will 4-21-1709, pr. 7-16-1709. Chd. John, Joseph, Benjamin, Thomas, Sarah Huggins, and Hanna.‡

Hall, Clement, s of Judge William Hall, who emig. in 1677, was b in Salem 30th of 6tn mo., 1706. Wf. Sarah; chd. Ann and William.‖
Clement. Wf. Margaret; chd. Prudence, b 9-29-1746; Elizabeth, b

8-14-1749, buried 8-14-1749; Morris, b 9-26-1750, buried 11-6-1750; William, b 2-20-1752, buried 9-21-1752; Clement, b 11-13-1753; Sarah, b 4-14-1755; Joseph, b 2-5-1757; Joseph, b 11-19-1760; Morris, b 10-13-1762; Margaret, b 1-18-1765, buried 10-16-1765.†

Clement, Esq., Salem, will 10-30-1741, pr. 6-7-1742. Wf. Elizabeth; chd. William, John, Anne (under age), and Ashton; bros. Nathaniel and William Hall; uncle Clement Plumstead; cousin William Plumstead.‡

John, m Ann Johnson, 6-11-1741.¶

John, int. 5-16-1747. Wf. Anne.‡

Margaret, wid. of Clement, and dau of Joseph and Prudence Morris, b 1-13-1722/3, d 9-21-1786.†

Samuel, shopkeeper, Salem Town, will 8-3-1742, affirmed 8-19-1742. Bros. John and Daniel Hall.‡

Sarah, Piles Grove, wid. Bond of adm. 3-2-1723/4.**

Thomas. Wf. Mary; chd. Thomas, b 1-7-1718/19; John, b 4-8-1716; Henry, b 12-4-1720/21.†

William, came as a servant of John Thompson: m a dau. of Thomas Pyle.††

William, m Elizabeth Pyle, 5-21-1684.¶

William, emig. 1677 from Dublin; m first, Elizabeth, dau of Thomas Pyle. Chd. Sorah, Hannah, Elizabeth, and Ann. He m second, Sarah Clement. Chd. William, Clement and Nathaniel.‖

William. Wf. Elizabeth; chd. Sarah, b 2-18-1689; Hannah, b 1-20-1692; Elizabeth, b 10-31-1694; Ann, b 9-19-1699; William, 8-22-1701; Clement, b 6-20-1706; Nathaniel, b 9-14-1709.†

William, merchant, Salem, will 4-10-1713, pr. 2-10-1713/14. Wf. Sarah; chd. Clement, William and Nathaniel (all under age); bro. Clement Plumsead ‡

William, son of William and Sarah (Clement) Hall, m Elizabeth, granddaughter of John Smith of Amblebury. Chd. Clement, b 15th of 12th mo., 1723; Sarah, b 1727; Susan, b 1728; Nathaniel, b 1730; Elizabeth, b 1735; Mary, b 1737; Edward, b 1740, m Ann, dau. of John and Ann (Nicholson) Brick‖

William, Alloways Creek, will 4-28-1728, pr. 5-28-1728. Chd. Daniel, John, Samuel, Sarah Roland, Mary and Hannah.§

Halladay, James, m Rains Condon, 6-23-1749.¶

Halton, Peter, planter, Fenwicks River, will 1-8-1691/2, rec. 7-6-1692. Wf. Mary; chd Frederick, Andrew and Bret'a.§

Hamilton, Archibald, schoolmaster, will 1-3-1746, pr. 12-22-1747. Wf. Judith; dau. Caterine Penton.§

Archibald, m Ann Robeson, 12-18-1746. Chd. William, bap. 7-9-1749.*

William, int. 11-22-1742. Wf. Mary.

Hammon, Richard, m Ann Turner, 1-28-1745.*

Hampton, John, Gloucester, m Ann Devall, Salem, 1-12-1736.¶

Hanby, William, Penns Neck, will 11-12-1702, rec. 12-30-1702. Wf. Jeane; chd. John, William, Richard and Daniel.§

Hancock, Edward, Alloways Creek, will 4-9-1739, affirmed 10-3-1739. Wf. Hanna; chd. Elizabeth, Hannah, Edward, Lidia and Grace (last three under age).‡

Isabella, wid. of William, shoemaker, Alloways Creek, will 9-1-1680. Sister Penticost Dixon and her daughter Hester Dixon, both of Old Brough, near Burrough Bridge, Yorkshire.§

Job, tailor, int. 10-23-1744.‡

John, of London, came to West Jersey abt. 10-25-1679, in the Willing Mind; m Mary, dau. of Nathaniel Champney, Sr., who with her mother came in the ship Henry and Ann, and ar. in the latter part of 7th mo., 1681, and settled on Alloways Creek. Chd. John, b 9-10-1690; William, b 11-1-1693; Elizabeth, b 6-12-1695.†

John. Wf. Mary; chd. Mary, b 4-15-1698; Sarah, b 11-15-1701; Nathaniel and Edward (twins) b 1-20-1703; Joseph, b 12-8-1704; Hannah, b 8-10-1706; Jonathan, 7-3-1708; Grace, b 5-20-1710.†

John, husb., Alloways Creek, d 2-26-1709. Wf. Mary; chd. John, William, Edward, Nathaniel, Joseph, Jonathan, Elixabeth, Mary Sarah and Hanneh‡

Mary, wid. Alloways Creek, inv. 4-13-1713.**

Nathaniel, Alloways Creek, will 11-5-1739, affirmed 5-1-1740. Dau. Mary (under age); mother-in-law Mary Chandler; bro.-in-law Joseph Stretch, Jr.‡

Richard, came in the Griffith, 1675.††

Richard, Cohanzick, inv. 5-29-1689.§

Richard, int. 12-18-1733‡

Samuel, int. 3-11-1740. Wf. Rebecca.‡

Samuel. Wf. Rebecca; chd. Richard, b 4-22-1727; Sarah, b 7-26-1729; Easter, b 4-14-1731; Elizabeth, b 7-24-1736; Samuel, b 6-28-1738.†

William, came from Eng., 1677, with wf. Isabella and sons John and William.††

William. Wf. Sarah; chd. Thomas, b 12-5-1714; Rebeckah, b 9-18-1717.†

William, Jr., m Mabel Chambless, 11-28-1745.¶

Hans, George, m Patience Loper, 2-16-1747.*

Hannah, Michael, Fairfield, inv. 11-23-1703. Son Robert.§
Samuel, m Abigail Preston of Deerfield, 2-25-1740/1. Chd. Samuel, bap. 5-10-1746; James, bap 6-1-1749.*

Harding, John, freeholder and laborer, will 2-2-1687/8, rec. 5-8-1688. Son John "now supposed to be in England."§

Harris, Anna, Fairfield Precinct, wid. of Thomas Harris. Chd. Thomas, Caleb, Jeremiah, and Sarah, wf of Thomas Ogden; granddau. Anna Harris. Will 12-13-1750, pr. 12-27-1750.‡

Isaac, int. 5-22-1745. Marcey Harris, adm.‡

Isaac, Deerfield. Wf. Mercy; chd Mary, bap. 6-7-1741; Hester, bap. 10-3-1743.*

Thomas, Fairfield Precinct, will 10-24-1749, pr. 12-20 (year not mentioned). Wf. Anna; chd. Caleb, Jeremiah, Isaac who has daus. Anna, Mercy, Mary and Esther; Thomas who has sons Isaac and Thomas (both under age); and Sarah Ogden.‡

Harrison, Israel, Munmouth Precinct, m Esther, dau. of Christopher and Esther White.||
Israel. Wf. Hester; dau. Sarah, b 12-14-1696.†
Israel, Munmouth River, husb., inv. 4th of 1st mo. (March), 1697/8. Wf. Hester.§

Hart, Dennis, m Ann Clark, 5-31-1749.*
Jane, ward, upwards of 14 yrs., dau. of John Hart, 3-25-1735.‡
Jane, spinster, int. 9-2-1738.§
Jane, spinster, int. 3-3-1748.‡
John. Wf. Ann; dau Jane, b 1-6-1719/20.†
John, merchant, Salem, will 4-20-1726, pr. 4-27-1726. Dau. Jeane under age); sister Jeane Hart, living near Glasco, Scotland; bro. William Hart; cousin Robert Hart.‡
Robert, merchant, Salem Town, will 9-13-1745, pr. 10-15-1745. Wf. Jane; chd. John, William, Lilly and Joseph.‡

Harvey, Edward, m Mary Aurey, 1-5-1749.¶

Haslewood, George, Salem, will 4-11-1693, rec. 6-27-1693. Wf. Margrett; son John; son-in-law (?stepson) Richard Butcher.§
John, Alloways Creek, will 10-14-1694, rec. 11-15-1694. Wf. Anne; father-in-law Samuel Curtice.§
Margaret, wid., will 11-20-1695. Son Richard Butcher.§

Hawke, Hezekiah, Pilesgrove, int. 12-21-1742. Wf. Johanna.‡

Haynes, Ann, wid., Salem Town, int. 3-26-1750.‡

Benjamin, weaver, will 1-15-1723, Affirmed 6-2-1733. Wf. Ann, chd. Joseph, Mary Ann (under age). Benjamin, John and Hannah; bro. Joseph Haynes.‡

Benjamin, carpenter. Salem Town, int. 6-29-1747.‡

Daniel, carpenter, Salem Town, int. 6-23-1740 Wf. Hannah.‡

John, husb., Mannington, will 6-28-1714, pr. 3-23-1714/15. Wf. Sarah; chd. Daniel, William, Sarah and Hannah.‡

John, m Rebecca Smith, 11-4-1745.¶

John, Salem Town, int. 3-26-1750.‡

Thomas, m Jane Brown, 3-23-1749.*

Healey, Henry. Wf. Mary; dau. Sarah, b 7-21-1793/4.†

Hedge, Nathan, tailor, Salem Town, will 5-5-1733, affirmed 8-15 1733. Mother, Rebecca Cox.‡

Samuel, came in the Griffith, 1675; in the spring of 1676 he m Ann, youngest dau. of John Fenwick.††

Samuel, Jr., Salem, will 2-5-1708/9, pr. 7-15-1709. Wf. Rebeck; chd Samuel Fenwick, William, Nathan and John; father Samuel Hedge.‡ and §

Samuel, Cohansey, will 5-12-1731. pr. 3-2-1731. Wf. Ann; chd. Samuel and Rebecca; mother Rebecca Cox; father Samuel Hedge; bros. Nathan Hedge, William Hedge, dec'd, and John Hedge, dec'd.‡

William, Munmouth River, husb., inv. 29th of 6th mo. (Aug.), 1702. Sister Dorcas Smith.§

William, weaver, Salem, will 3-5-1728/9 pr. 3-26-1729. Mother Rebecca Cox; Brother Samuel Hedge.‡

Heins, Lawrence, comb maker, int. 1-12-1743.§

Hendrickson, Laucey, Penns Neck' non. will 10 12-1700. Bro. in-law Gilljohn Gilljohnson, and 4 sisters not named.§

Laurance (alias Lacy), Sr., Finns Point, planter, will 2-10-1686/7, pr. 6-15-1687. Wf. Mary; s Laurence (alias Lacy).§

Hern, William, Cumb. Co., will 5-3-1749, pr. 5-17-1749.‡

Hewes, Edward, Oldmans Creek, will 5th of 10th mo. (Dec.), 1739. Wf. Hannah; chd. Elihu, Benjamin, Tabitha and Hannah (all under age); bros. Aaron, Joseph and James Hews.‡

Thomas, Oldmans Creek, will 25th of 2d mo. (Apr.), 1735, affirmed 5-26-1735. Wf. Mary; chd. Joseph, Thomas, and 1 chd. not named; bro. Edward Hewes.‡

William, Oldmans Creek, will 7th of 2d mo (Apr.), 1733, pr. 5-22-1733. Wf. Sarah; chd, Ruth, Edward and Thomas.‡

Hewins, Thomas, m Rachel Dickson, 8-13-1745.¶

Hews, James. Wf. Jane; dau. Jane, b 8-9-1737.+

Hide (Hyde), **Thomas,** carpenter, Munmouth River, will 2-5-1688/9, rec. 7-30-1689.§

Hill, Aaron. Son Moses, bap. 7-27-1744.*
Sarah, wid. Adm. granted 8-17-1726, to Elizabeth, wid. of Thomas Hill.‡
Thomas. Wf. Elizabeth; chd. Elizabeth, b 12-1-1714; Thomas, b 4-17-1715; Rebeckah, b 12-13-1719; Hannah, b 9-17-1722; Sarah, b 6-31-1725.†
Thomas, merchant, Salem. Bond of Elizabeth Hill as Adm. 11-1-1725.‡
Thomas, Esq., Salem Town, will 9-24-1741, affirmed 10-22-1741. Wf. Margaret; dau. Elizabeth (under age); sisters Rebecca, Hannah and Sarah Hill; cousin Samuel Mason who has daus. Sarah and Elizabeth Mason; bros.-in-law Isaac and Joseph Sharp.‡

Histis, Walter, Penns Neck, will 6-3-1707, pr. 4-13-1708. Chd. James; son-in-law William; dau.-in-law Mary (?stepchildren).‡

Hodge, Abraham, Cohansie, will 5-25-1712, pr. 6-24-1712. Wf. Anna; dau. Mary; sister Elizabeth; brothers Joseph and Benjamin.**
Bernard, m Elizabeth Prague, 1-1-1688.¶
Bernard, Cesariae River, will 28th of 9th mo. (Nov.), 1694, rec. 2-6-1694/5. Wf. Elizabeth; chd. Abraham, Elizabeth, Joseph, Benjamin.**
Joseph, m Mary Shaw, 4-5-1746.¶

Hoeman, Jasper, laborer, inv.10-8-1701. Bro.-in-law Samuel Hunter.§

Hoffman (Hopman), **Andrew,** Pilesgrove, will 9-29-1725, pr. 5-8-1728. Wf. Mary; chd. Mounce, Catherine, Mary, Beata, Rebekah, Margaret, Susannah, Magdalene, Laurence, John and Andrew.‡
Andrew, int. 8-12-1745. Wf. Catheron.‡

Hogben, Nehemiah, m Hannah Bowin, 12-6-1744.¶

Holbrook, John, ship carpenter, int. 7-12-1736.‡

Holme, Benjamin, m Jean Smith, 12-24-1750.¶
Benjamin, Jr.. m Hannah Holme, 12-24-1750.¶
John, came from England. Son John.∥
John, s of John. Chd. John, Elizabeth, wf. of Joseph Fogg; and Benjamin, b about 1730.∥

Holmes, Israel, m Mary Peterson, 12-14-1729.‡
John, Munmouth River, will 1-17-1703/4, pr. 2-4-1703/4. Chd.

John, Samuel, Benjamin, Hannah and Elizabeth; son-in-law, Nicholas Moore; bro.-in-law Samuel Hedge, Sr.‡

Jonathan, Cohansey, will 9-15-1715, pr. 9-28-1715. Wf. Susannah; chd. Janathan, Obadiah, Samuel (all under age), Elizabeth and Susannah; father Obadiah Holmes; bros. Noah Miller and Samuel Holmes.‡

Obadiah, Cohansey, inv. 6-10-1723. Wf. Hannah.**

Obadiah, int. 7-12-1735.‡

Samuel, Greenwich, will 3-10-1749/50, pr. 3-28-1750. Cousins Jonathan Holmes and Obadiah Robbins.‡

Holsten, Andrew, m Elizabeth Royall, 8-21-1736.¶

Holstin, (Holstein) **Larans,** (Lorance), Pilesgrove, will 8-23-1742, pr. 1-26-1750. Chd. Lorance, Mathias, Andrew, Elizabeth, Mary, Sarah and Susana.‡

Holton, Charles, husb., Penns Neck, int. 1-18-1738.‡

John, m Elizabeth Elweel, 1-25-1745.¶

Hopman, Charles, Pilesgrove, inv. 8-18-1719.**

John, will 2-4-1714/15, pr. 6-29-1715. Chd. Brigit, John, Nicholas, Mounce, Miccahel, and others not named; bro. Frederick Hopman.‡

John, Morrise River, will 4-26-1746, pr. 5-6-1748. Wf. Cathren; chd. John, Frederick, Peter, Jonas and Gabriel.‡

Hopper, John, ward, son of Benjamin Hopper, weaver, Alloways Creek, 8-5-1734.‡

Horsel, Ruben, int. 8-5-1742.‡

Horsford, Samuel, int. 5-11-1744.**

Horsely, Ralfe, d 12-4-1699. Wf. Mary.§

Hoskins, Cesar, husb., Prince Morrises River, inv. 3-2-1726/7.‡

John, husb., Morris River, d 12-16-1728. Sarah Hoskins, adm.**

Houlstone, William, planter, Stowe Creek, non. will 11-21-1692. Wf. Elianor.

Howell, Charles, farmer, Cohansie, int. 11-24-1742. Son Charles; bro. John Howell, Jr., of Southampton, L. I.‡

Huckings, Hester, wid., will 10-19-1697, rec. 8-6-1697/8. Chd. Roger, John, Mary, Hester Sikes and Sarah.§

Roger, Alloways Creek, non. will 12-23-1689. Wf. Hester; chd. Roger, John, and Mary, wf. of John Alin.§

Roger. Wf. Sarah; chd. Hannah, b 10-10-1707; Sarah, b 8-24-1709, Acsah, b 1-15-1711/12; Elizabeth, b 11-19-1713; Susannah, b 3-12-1715;

Huldah, b 1-3-1717/18; Hindrance, b 1-1-1719; Thomas, b 2-28-1728.†

Huddy, Daniel. Wf. Elizabeth; chd. Joshua, b 11-8-1735; Martha, b 5-29-1742; Daniel, b 6-15-1747.†

Hudley, Daniel, m Elizabeth Booth, 6-24-1732.¶

Hudson, Abraham Cohansey, will 12-23-1732, inv. 1-10-1732/3. Wf. Deborah; chd. Joshua, Benjamin (under age), Lydia; bro. Isaac Hudson.‡

Isaac, m Rachel Weaten, 6-11-1733.¶

Richard, int. 12-28-1737.‡

William, planter, Cesariae River, inv. 1-12-1687. Wf. Mary.§

Hues (Hughs), **John,** Mannington Precinct, will 4-23-1710, pr. 3-24-1714/15. Wf Martha; chd. John and Jonathan.‡

Huestis, Moses, carpenter, Amwelbury, non. will 11-16-1694. Father Robert Heustis of Westchester, N. Y.§

Hughes, Edward. Wf. Hannah; chd. Tabitha, b 7-29-1727; Elihu, b 11-16-1725; Benjamin, b 12-17-1728.†

John, int. 1-7-1747.‡

Thomas, m Mary Pedrick, 5-11-1727.¶

Hulbert (Hurlbert), **Edward.** tailor, will 8-28-1698, rec. 9-28-1698. Wf. Rebeckah; son-in-law (?stepson) Joseph Hill, whose mother was Agnes Hill §

Humphrey, John. Wf. Rachel; chd. Ann, bap. 10-25-1741.*

Hunt, John, m Sarah Darkin, 9-6-1743.¶

William. Wf. Sarah; chd. William, b 4-18-1723; Thomas, b 12-17-1728.†

William, husb. will 4-10-1727, pr. 2-14-1740. Wf. Sarah; chd. John, William, Thomas, Ann, Sarah and Elizabeth (all under age except John).‡

Hunter, Richard, tanner, late of Dublin, Ire., now of West Jersey, will 7ber (Sept.) 8, 1697. Wf. Elizabeth; chd. Benjamin, Ann, Rachell and Elizabeth.§

Samuel m Katherine Skeene, 10-31-1695.¶

William, weaver, Cesariae River, will 4-23-1690, rec. 9-23-1690. Son Samuel §

Hurley, Henry, weaver, Manenton Creek, inv. 2-26-1694/5. Wf. Mary.§

Husson (Husten), **William,** will 1-22-1720/21, pr. 8-14-1722. Wf. Ann; son William (under age).‡

Hustis, Walter, Penns Neck, will 6-30-1707, pr. 4-2-1708. Chd.

James (under age), William and John; son-in-law William; dau-in-law Mary.*†

Hutchings, Hugh, m Mary Adams, 2-3-1686/7.¶

Isard, Michael, Greenwich, inv. 14th of 10th mo. (Dec.), 1694. Wf. Mary.§

Jackson, James. Wf. Sarah Ann; s Joseph, bap. 4-17-1743.*

Jacob, John, Salem Creek, will 11-11-1685, rec. 1-12-1687/8. Wf. Barbara.§

Jaffrey, John, merchant, Salem Town, will 1-19-1703/4, pr. 2-24-1703/4. Dau. Jean; bro. Alexander Jaffrey, merchant in Sterling, Scotland.‡

Jagger, Daniel. Wf. Martha; chd. David and Rachel, bap. 1-30-1742/3.*

David. Wf. Mary; chd. Jemima, bap. 7-22-1744; Deborah, bap. 4-26-1746/7.*

David. Wf. Martha; chd. Deborah, bap. 4-23-1747; Dorothy, bap. 9-3-1749.*

John. Wf. Elizabeth; chd. Elizabeth, bap. 11-1-1741.*

Jonathan. Wf. Elizabeth; chd. Abner and Phebe, both bap. 8-24-1740; John, bap. 7-8-1744; Jonathan, bap. 4-20-1746; Eunice, bap. 5-29-1748.*

James, Joseph, Cumberland, m Margaret Butler, 2-1-1748.¶

Janes (Jeans), **Henry,** Swart Hook, Penns Neck, inv. 2-8-1692/3. Wf. Mary.§

Jaquat, John, Penns Neck, will 11-19-1747, pr. 12-5-1747. Chd. Paul, Peter, Rebecca, Mary, wf. of Joseph Elwell; Hance and Joseph (last 2 under age) ‡

Peter, Penns Neck, will 12-23-1748, pr. 12-31-1748. Wf. Jane.‡

Jaquatt, Mary, wid of Paul, Penns Neck, will 6-22-1702, rec. 4-16-1703.§

Paul, Penns Neck, will rec. 12-9-1702. Wf. Mary; chd. John, Paul, Peter, Casperus, Mary and Sarah; bro. John who has sons Peter and Cornelius.§

Jarman (Germon), **John,** blacksmith, Salem, will 3-4-1735; pr. 1-22-1738. Wf. Martha.‡

Jeanes, Henry, will 3-18-1737, pr. 3-1-1737/8. Chd. Henry, Anna, Jeane, Christiana, Margaret (daus. under age); cousins John and Mary Test; bros. Joseph Test and Matthias Lambson ‡

John, Penns Neck, inv. 12-1-1712. Chd. Brigit and Mary.

Nathaniel, Penns Neck, will 2-5 1702/3. Chd. Henry (under age), daus. not named; bro. John.§

Jeffrey, John. Wf. Gertrude; dau. Jane, b 10-11-1703.†

Jelley, George, inv. 3-10-1714/15.**

Jenkins, Nathaniel, m Ruth Sayre, 4-21-1743.¶

Jennens, James, Deerfield Twp., int. 10-24-1749. Wf. Rebecca.‡

Jennings, Henry, s of Willam and Mary, b Parish of Clemond Deane, County Surry, Eng., m Margaret, dau. of Paul Busse, of York City, Eng., 1-18-1666; lived in Thames Ditton, near Kingston on Thames; sailed 2-5-1677, in the "Kent," arriving 6-23-1677.†

Mary, Elsinburrow, wid., will 3-30-1749, pr. 4-6-1749. Son-in-law James Jennings; dau-in-law Margaret Jennings; granddau. Jean Dickey; son Robert Dickey.

Redmon, Pilesgrove, int. 9-10-1748. Mary Jennings, adm.*‡

Richard, m Ann Atkinson, 4-18-1734.‡

Jequat (Jaquet,)**Peter,** carpenter, will 12-27-1721, pr. 1-25-1721/2. wf. Sarah ‡

Jewell, John, Salem, will 3-9-1705/6, pr. 3-19-1729/30. Wf. Ann.‡

John, cordwainer, Salem, will 2d of 12th mo. 1726/7, pr. 2-6-1726/7. Wf. Margaret.‡

Johnson, Andrew, Penns Neck, bond of adm. 4-11-1730.**

Ard, planter, inv. 9-29-1687.§

Clause, Penns Neck, will 12-1-1701, rec. 6-17-1702. Wf. Elizabeth; chd. John and others not named.§

Erick, Penns Neck, int. 2-17-1746/7. Margaret Johnson, adm.‡

Erock, Penns Neck, will 1-1-1712/13. Wf. Cathrien; chd. Mathis and William.‡

Ezeckel, Penns Neck, inv. 11-29-1726.‡

John, Penns Neck, will 2-15-1719/20, pr. 1-3-1720/1. Chd. Class and Mary, (both under age.)**

John, husb., Mannington Precinct, will 4-2-1728, pr. 5-1-1728. Wf. Sarah; chd. John, Catrin Brown, and Henry.‡

John, Mannington, int. 3-10-1732.‡

Margaret, Salem, wid. of Robert Johnson, will 8-18-1730, pr. 9-3-1730. Chd. Mary Johnson, Joseph Sears (under age), Richard Sears, Robert Johnson, Anne Johnson.**

Martin, Penns Neck, will 2-5-1729/30, pr. 4-11-1730. Wf. Elizabeth; chd. Nicholas, Garret, Margaret, Elizabeth and Susanna.‡

Mathias, Penns Neck. Acct. of estate, 1730.**

Nicholas, Cohansey, will 9-1-1732, pr. 2-27-1732/3. Wf. Mary; chd. Nicholas, Othniel, Nathaniel, Sarah Haries, Hannah Peterson, Ann Smith, Temperance and Sarah (last 2 under age).‡

Nicholas, Penns Neck, will 11-28-1744, pr. 12-6-1744. Bro. Garret Johnson.‡

Paul, Maurice River, int. 11-5-1748. Rebecca Johnson, adm.‡

Rhina, spinster, int. 1-10-1733 ‡

Richard, came from Surry, Eng.; m Mary Grover, 25th of 6th mo., 1682, at Salem. He d 1st mo. 1719; his wf., Mary, d in 1714. Chd. Robert, Elizabeth m John Pierson and d in 1720; Anna, b 1687, m Alexander Grant in 1714.∥

Richard, Salem, will 1-18-1719/20, pr. 2-2-1719/20. Chd. Robert, and Elizabeth Pearson; granddaus. Elizabeth Pearson and Mary Johnson.‡

Robert, s of Richard and Mary Johnson, m Margaret, wid. of Joseph Sayre in 1717. He d 13th of 12th mo., 1728; Margaret d in 1730, aged 37 yrs. Chd. Robert, Mary and Ann.∥

Robert, Salem, will 12-13-1728, pr. 4-8-1728/9. Wf. Margaret; chd. Robert, Mary, Ann and Elizabeth (all under age) sons-in-law (?stepsons) Joseph and Richard Siers; neice Elizabeth Pearson.**

Thomas, Manenton Creek, will last day of 7th mo. (Sept.), 1696, rec. 10-13-1696. Chd. Thomas and Sarah (both under age); bro. Richard Johnson.§

William, Cesariae River, alias Cohansie, tailor, will 5-6-1694, rec. 1-5-1694/5. Wf Frances; chd. Samuel and William (both under age).§

William, Maninton Precinct. Adm. granted 3-24-1723/4.‡

Jones, Andrew, Fairfield Precinct, int. 3-24-1747/8.***

John, Cohansey, will 11-11-1735, pr. 11-5-1135. Wf. Hannah; chd. John, Samuel, Elizabeth, Andrew, Joseph and Elinor, wf. of Samuel Barnes.‡

John, schoolmaster. Salem, will 10 26-1739, pr. 11-5-1739. Wf. Mary; son John; son-in-law Job Hancock.‡

John, innkeeper, Salem, will 4-16-1740, pr. 5-2-1740. Wf Elizabeth; mother Mary Jones; sisters Elinor Jenkins of Bristol, Elizabeth Jones and Ann Mullin of Philadelphia.‡

Marcus, int. 6-24-1749 ‡

Thomas, m Hannah Prior, 4-12-1687 ¶

Thomas, Penns Neck, inv. 8-16-1694. Wf. Hannah.§

Jordan (Jarden), **James,** Mannington Precinct, husb., will 11-8-1729. Wf. Hannah.**

Joyce, Henry, Greenwitch, will 3-8-1725/6.‡

Joyner, Peter. Wf. Jane; chd Mary, bap. 5-21-1749.*

Jureson (Juranson, Jurinson, Jurians), **Stephen,** Pompion Hook, Penns Neck, will 10-14-1700. Wf. Christian, Hendrick's daughter; chd. Ann, Katherine, George and Henry; dau-in-law (?stepdau.) Bridget.§

Justin, Andrew, will 7-15-1740, pr. 8-19-1740. Chd. Ann Corneliuson and Catherin Willin; grandchd. Marey Scott and Elinor Willin.‡

Kasbey, Edward. Wf. Elizabeth; chd. Mary, b 10-3-1703; Edward, b 3-11-1705; Mathew, b 10-4-1730.†

Keasbey, Edward, emig. from England. Wf. Elizabeth, wid. of Isaac Smart and dau. of Andrew and Isabella Thompson, b near Dublin, Ire., 15th of 8th mo. 1666. Chd. Mary, Edward, m Elizabeth. dau. of Edward Bradway, Jr.; Mathew, and Susanna.‖

Edward, Salem Town, will 8-13-1712, pr. 12-24-1712. Wf. Elizabeth; chd. Edward and Matthew.§

Edward. Wf. Elizabeth; chd. Edward, b 3-22-1726; Mary, b 1-14-1727/8; Bradway, b 10-4-1730.†

Edward, Salem, will 2-9-1733/4, affirmed 3-8-1733/4. Chd. Broadway, Edward and Mathew (all under age); bro. Matthias Keasbey.‡

Mathew. Wf. Sarah; chd. Sarah, b 10-21-1730; Mary, b 2-24-1733; Elizabeth, b 12-2-1734/5; John, b 9-13-1736.†

Mathew, joiner, Salem, will 10th of 10th mo. (Dec.), 1737, affirmed 12-31-1737. Wf. Sarah; chd. John and Mary (both under age).‡

Keen, Erick, Maurice River Twp., int. 4-30-1750. Wf. Catherain.‡
Jonas, int. 9-11-1750.§
Peter, m Elizabeth Bassett, 6-20-1747.¶

Kelahan, John, Penns Neck, will 2-24-1749/50, pr. 9-3-1750. Wf. Margaret; chd. Marey, John and Margaret.‡

Kelley, Thomas, will 3-12-1728/9, pr. 3-29-1729. Wf. Rachel; chd. John, Thomas, Mary, Martha and James.‡

Kent, Erasimus, Maninton Precinct, bricklayer, will 7-14-1723, inv. 7-15-1723. Wf. Elizabeth; chd. Erasimus, Thomas, and Edmund.‡ and §

Erasmus, m Ann Eaton, 2-17-1747.¶

Thomas, planter, Salem, will 14th of 2d mo. (Apr.), 1691, rec. 5-22-1691. Wf. Ann; chd. Robert, Thomas, Erasmus, Sarah (last 3 under age).§

Kenton, William, carpenter, late of Maryland, now of Salem, will 12-8-1693, rec. 4-23-1694. Wf. Mary; chd. William and John (both under age).§

Kerr, John, int. 9-13-1742. Wf. Sarah.**

Kidd, John, Mannington, will 10-16-1750, pr. 1-25-1750/51. Chd. Abraham, Isaac, William, whose wf. is Ann; Jacob, Ann wf. of Edward Johnson; Elizabeth, wf. of James Halton; Mary; wf. of John Wood.‡

Killingsworth, Prudence, wid. Thomas, will 4-21-1709, pr. 8-26-1709.‡ and §

Thomas, Salem Town, will 7-10-1705. Wf. Prudence.‡ and §

Kinish, John, m Barbara Barn, 2-7-1749.*

Knowles, Thomas, planter, New Salem, inv. 4-4-1682.§

Lecroy, Machiel (Machielse), planter, Lacroy's Point, will 5-19-1685, pr. 2-10-1686/7. Wf. Margrett, Lucas' daughter.§

Lambson, Joseph, tailor, Penns Neck Bond of adm. 7-30-1723.‡
Thomas, and wf. Ann, came to America and located in Penns Neck in 1690.††
Thomas, Penns Neck, will 12-19-1735, pr. 1-4-1735. Wf. Ann; chd. Mathias, Michael, Daniel, Elenor Pennington, Thomas, and Mary Elwell.‡

Langley, Thomas, int. 3-27-1735. Wf. Mary.‡

Langstaff, Laban, m Ann Hewit, 12-21-1744.*

Langton, Thomas, m Ruth Wright, 1-15-1746.¶

Lazilier, Michel. Bond of adm. 4-21-1717.—*Administration Bonds 1716-1756.*

Leatherland, Joseph, Mannington, laborer, inv 3-9-1727/8.**

Leckey, Thomas, int. 2-13-1748/9.‡

Lecroy, John, m Bridget Darby, 5-30-1749.*

Leek, Recompence, Deerfield, will 3-30-1749, pr. 11-18-1749. Wf. Martha; chd. John, Samuel, Recompence, Nathan, Abigail, Elizabeth, Sarah, Rachel, Hannah (daus. under age).‡

Lefevor, Hipolite, Salem, inv. 2-4-1697. Son-in-law John Worlidge.§

Lestrang, James, weaver, Manington, int. 11-7-1748.‡

Lewis, John, Elsenburgh, will 6th of 4th mo. (June), 1712. Wf. Jeal; chd. Jonathan, Joseph. Lewis, David. Joshua, Sarah and Jane Morris (stepchd.). Pr. 5-1-1713.**
John, m Mary Burden, 11-18-1730.¶

John, husb., Manington; will 2-15-1742/3, affirmed 3-26-1743. Wf Ruth; chd. Joseph (under age), Sarah, Elizabeth, Mary, John.‡
William, lab., Elsenburgh. Bond of adm. 11-29-1734.§

Linch, Elinor, wid., Penns Neck, inv 2-5-1712/13.**
Samuel, m Sarah Pedrick, 9-10-1730.¶

Lindsey, Margret, Allawaies Creek, dau. of Thomas Lindsey, late of Elk River, Cecil Co., Md., will 5-10-1708, pr. 5-1-1712.**

Lippincott, Freedom. Wf. Elizabeth; chd. Samuel, b 12-12-1728.†

Lloyd, Ephraim, m Anne Walker, 5-18-1746.¶
Obadiah. Chd. Hester, bap. 5-12-1741.*

Locroy (Locry, Lecroy), **John,** husb. Penns Neck, will 3-23-1727/8, pr. 4-5-1728/9. Chd. Michael, Lucas, Jane Butler, Sarah Hogben, Mary Lord, John.‡

Lodge, Benjamin, Salem, m Sarah Fisher, Gloucester, 10-15-1742.¶

Long, Elihu, Mannington, will 3-15-1748/9, affirmed 4-3-1749. Chd. Abner, Daniel, Malachi, Rebecca.‡
William, husb., will 11-14-1743, pr. 1-10-1743/4. Chd. Joseph, Elihu, Elizabeth, wf. of Abraham Cunningham.§

Loper, Arthur, cooper, will 4-30-1720, pr. 6-13-1720. Wf. Patiace; Chd. David, Arthur, Thurston, John, James, William, Jonatnan, Phebe (all except David under age).‡

Lorance, Nathan, Cohansey, will 11-23-1744, pr. 4-24-1745. Wf. Elizabeth; chd. Rhoda, Violetta, Abigail, wf. of Daniel Elmore; Jonathan, Nathan, Elizabeth Shephard.‡

Lord, Abraham, m Anicka Mullicka, 4-2-1736.¶
Joseph, int. 1-8-1734. Wf. Alice.‡

Louden (Lowden), **Reniere,** tailor, Pilesgrove Precinct, will 3-26-1730, pr. 4-14-1730. Wf. Easter; chd. Robard, Rachel and Eales.**

Love, Robert and Mary, wards, 12-3-1739.§

Low, John, Penns Neck, inv. 10-7-1729.**

Loyd, John, Pilesgrove, will 1-23-1727/8, pr. 10-7-1728. Chd. Obadiah, John and Joseph.**
John, Pilesgrove, will 5-4-1730, pr. 6-3-1730. Wf. Katherine; chd. John, Bateman and Obediah.**

Obediah, lab., inv. 2-2-1695/6. Bro. Joseph Loyd.§

Lumley, Edward, Alloways Creek. Wf. Sarah; chd. Rebekah and John, bap. 8-13-1747; Edward, bap. 11-1-1747.*

Lummis, Edward, m Margaret Elmer, 1737.¶
Edward, Cohansey, will 10-28-1738, pr. 5-5-1740. Wf. Abigail; chd. Edward, Abigail, Samuel, Sarah, Daniel, Mary, Tamson and Lydia.‡

MacClang, James. Wf. Ann; dau. Mary, bap. 8-10-1740.*

Maddocks, John, s of Ralph, b at Chesshire, Eng., abt. 1638; re to London 1688; m 1669, Elizabeth Burnham, wid. of Ralph. In 1671 dau. Elizabeth was b at St. Pluchers, London. In 1678 John, wf. Elizabeth and dau. Elizabeth, with his son-in-law (?stepson), Richard Burnham and manservants Thomas Oads and Thomas Hooten and maidservant Sarah Wagstafe, sailed in the "Success," arriving in Virginia in December, and at Salem in January following. Elizabeth, dau. of John and Elizabeth, m James Denn and had two chd., Margaret, b 4-29-1689, and John, b 6-11-1693.†

John, Alloways Creek, will 14th of 11th mo., 1700/1, rec. 3-22-1700/1. Dau. Elizabeth Powell, who has chd. John Maddocks Denn, Margaret Denn, Mary Powell and Elizabeth Powell; son-in-law Richard Burnham.§

Magogin, Alexander, int. 12-29-1742. Wf. Mary.‡

Maharr, Francis, m Elizabeth Casperson, 12-11-1745.¶

Maiden, John, husb., inv. 12-30-1697.§

Mains, Samuel (Maynes), int, 1-6-1734. Wf. Anne.‡

Mall, Roger, Cohansey, will 5-8-1730, pr. 1-18-1744. Wf Ellenor; chd. George, Robert, Benjamin, Joseph and Roger (last 2 under age).‡

Mallally, Bryant, int. 10-21-1749.‡

Man (Mann), **John,** merchant. Bond of adm. 10-28-1727.‡

March, John, non: will 6-1-1695. inv. 23d of 7th mo. (Sept.) 1717.§

Marshall, Daniel, Elsenburgh, lab., will 11th ot 7th mo. (Sept.), 1697. Father Thomas Marshall; bros. Thomas, John and Samuel Marshall; sisters Elizabeth and Sarah; cousin John Thompson. Jr.§

John, m Elizabeth Sparks, 1-5-1741/2. Chd. Simon, bap. at Woodbury, 4-25-1746.*

Mary, spinster, Alloways Creek, will 5-5-1735, affirmed 5-14-1735. Nephews Isaac, Thomas and Richard Moss sister Rebeckah's chd.; Elizabeth Blancher; bro. Abraham Moss.‡

Richard, Alloways Creek, will 1-7-1718/19, pr. 12-8-1719. Wf. Sarah;

Chd. Richard, Thomas, Rebecca and Mary (last 2 under age).‡
Thomas, Alloways Creek, inv. 5-16-1728.**
William, int. 2-7-1748/9. Elizabeth Marshall, adm.‡

Martin, John, int. 2-4-1741. Wf. Sarah.‡

Marvel, Joseph, int. 9-21-1735.‡

Maskell, Constant, Cohansey, int. 1-5-1739. Wf. Rachel.
Thomas, Cohansey, will 10-26-1732, affirmed 1-30-1732. Wf Mary; Chd. Mary Yuens, Constant; grandchd. Maskell Yuens.‡

Mason, Aaron, Manningngton, farmer, will 30th of 8th mo. (Oct), 1734, affirmed 11-6-1734. Wf. Abigail; chd. Thomas, Joseph and Samuel; father Thomas Mason.‡
Aaron. Wf. Abigail; chd. Samuel, b 10-10-1731; Sarah, b 11-8-1734.†
James, Cesariae River, husb., inv. 11-20-1702. Wf. Mary.§
John, of Gloucestershire, Eng., emig. 1683; m Sarah, dau. of John Smith. Chd. John, Ann, William, Sarah, Samuel, Thomas and Rebecca.‖
John. Wf. Sarah; chd. John, b 7-19-1697; Ann, b 11-24-1699; William, b 11-23-1701; Sarah, b 2-2-1704; Samuel, b 3-15-1706; Thomas, b 5-28-1708; Rebecca, b 9-6-1710.†
John, Elsenburgh, will 12-6-1725, pr. 4-14-1726. Chd. John, Samuel, Thomas and Rebecka; granddau. Hannah Darkin; son-in-law Joseph Darkin.‡
John, int. 5-15-1749.‡
Samuel. Wf. Elizabeth; chd. Sarah, b 9-25-1732.†
Samuel, Elsenborough, will 12-16-1744. pr. 2-11-1744. Wf. Grace; chd. Sarah, Elizabeth; bro. John Mason, who has daus. Anne and Mary.‡
Thomas came from England abt the time his bro. John came (1683). He first resided at Salem; later in Mannington.††
Thomas. Wf. Elizabeth; chd. Mary, b 7-2-1701; Aaron, b 7-2-1702; Martha, b 9-12-1704; Joseph, b 3-14-1706; Jonathan, b 11-15-1707; James, b 6-11-1709.†
Thomas, Mannington, will 8th of 10th mo. (Dec.) 1728, pr. 6-11-1729. Wf. Elizabeth; chd. Aaron, who has sons Thomas and Joseph; James (under age), Mary Smith and Martha Wood.**
Thomas. Wf. Sarah; s John, b 10-16-1733.†
Thomas, formerly of Salem Co., now of Philadelphia, merchant, will 4-12-1738, affirmed 5-6-1740. Wf. Sarah; s John (under age); cousins Hannah and Sarah Darkin, and Ann and Mary Mason; bro. John Mason; bro-in-law Isaac Sharp.‡

Maule, Benjamin, Deerfield. Chd. Sarah, John, Hannah, Lydia, Benjamin, all bap. 4-14-1743; Rebekah, bap. 10-12-1746; Abigail, bap. 4-30 1749.*

Robert, Deerfield. Chd. Eleanor, bap. 1-25-1740/1.*

Mayhew, Thomas, m Hannah Rose, 5-13-1745. Chd. Uriah, bap. 7-27-1746; Israel, bap. 5-26-1748.*

Maysey, Richard, Manenton Creek, planter; inv. 12-2-1687.§

McCleese, Daniel, m Abigail Lumley, 2-18-1746.*

McClenan (McLanning), **Samuel,** m Mary Worldin (Woldin), 11-31-1741.¶

McDaniel, William, Cohansey, non. will 4-1-1726, inv. 4-25-1726.‡

McKeen, James, int. 3-2-1736. Wf. Katherine.—*East Jersey Wills, Liber B.*

John. Dau. Jane, bap. 2-28-1741/2.*

McKinne, Barnabas, m Ann Henry, 12-27-1748. Son William bap. 11-6-1749.*

McKnight, Hugh, int. 2-15 1732. Hannah McKnight, adm.‡
Malcolm, Penns Neck, tailor, will 8-22-1741, pr. 9-4-1741. Wf Cathren; chd. Charles, John, Malcolm and Susanna.‡

McLane, William, wheelwright, int. 10-15-1739.‡

McNichols, Daniel. Wf. Margaret; s. George, b 9-29-1707.†
George, Wf. Rebeckah; chd. Mary, b 8-13-1745; Hannah, b 5-1-1747; William, b 5-1-1749; Phebe, b 6-6-1751; Fathaniel, b 12-12-1753; Isaac, b 3-14-1756; John, b 4-25-1758; Andrew, b 12-24-1760; Rebeckah, b 7-19-1764.†

McWilliams, William, int. 6-8-1735.§

Meally, Hugh, int. 7-14-1741.‡

Mecum, William, Penns Neck, will 1-3-1747/8, pr. 3-5-1747. Chd William and Margaret (both under age).‡

Middleton, Hugh, will 1-19-1713, pr. 2-19-1713/14. Chd. John and Mary; dau.-in-law (?stepdau.) Sarah Hurley.‡

Miles, Thomas. Wf. Eleanor; wid. of Thomas Gilljohnson. Son Francis.‖
Thomas; weaver, Penns Neck, will 5-5-1743, pr. 5-21-1743. Chd. Francis (under age).‡

Miller, Alexander, m Hannah Jordan, 4-7-1730.‡

Ebenezer, s of Joseph Miller, m Sarah, dau. of John Collier (?). Chd. Ebenezer, b 15th of 9th mo., 1725, m Ruth Wood; Hannah, b 1728, m in 1740, Charles, son of Daniel Fogg; Josiah, b 1731; Andrew, b 1732; William, b 1735; John C , b 1737; Mark, b 1740; Sarah, b 1743; Rebecca, b 17th of 5th mo., 1747.‖

George, blacksmith Pilesgrove, will 2-18-1742, pr. 2-28-1742. Wf. Mary; chd, Joost and James (both under age); bro. William Miller.‡

James, tailor. Adm. granted 4-20-1723.‡

James, ward, 14 yrs. and upwards, s of George Miller, 2-8-1749.§

John. Wf. Margaret; chd. Catherine, bap. 4-9-1741; Jacob, bap. 4-8-1744; Abraham, bap. 5-3-1747; Elizabeth, bap. 5-6-1750.*

John, m Sarah Dickinson, 2-6-1741/2.*

John, cooper, Cohansey, will 9-12-1740. Wf. Susannah.***

John, int 3-26-1736. Wf. Martha.‡

John, Cesaria River. will 8-23-1699, pr. 11-3-1699. Wf. Mary; chd. Noah, John, Preserved, Mary, wf. of Thomas Stratton of Easthampton, L. I.; Susanna, wf. of Jonathan Holmes, and Hester Miller.‡

Joost. Wf. Christiana; chd. Mary, bap. 8-23-1741; Henry, bap. 2-5-1743/4; Elizabeth, bap. 4-27-1746; Catharine, bap 5-22, 1748; Rachel, bap. 10-28-1749/50.*

Joseph, surveyor. Son Ebenezer, b at Cohansey in 1702.‖

Noah, Cohansey, will 3-19-1725/6, pr. 10-8-1737. Wf. Joanah; chd. Samuel, Noah, John, Elizabeth, Joanna, and Susannah.‡

Noah, Cohansey, int. 10-30-1741. Wf. Susannah.‡

Ruth, wid., int. 10-23 1736.‡

Susannah, wid. of John, Cohansey, will 5-18-1749, pr. 6-3-1749. Chd. Elizabeth, Susanna, and Jonathan; son Jonathan Holmes.‡

Mills, James, tailor, int. 1-30-1738.‡

John, Indian Fields, will 4-12-1735, pr. 6-3-1735. Wf. Mary; chd. John, Seelye, Ephraim, Uriah, Jedidiah, Mary, Sarah, and Rebecca.‡

John, south side of Cohansey, called Rich Neck, will 3-10-1740/41, pr. 5-21-1741 Wf. Pheebe; chd. Jerediah and Jeremiah (both under age).‡

John, Stowe Creek, int. 2-22-1748. Wf. Mary.‡

Minck, Paul, Penns Neck, inv. 7-12-1696. Eldest son John.§

Mira, Jacob. Wf. Margaret; dau. Catharine, bap. 4-22-1749/50.*

Mire, Leonard, m Catharine Fisher, 11-24-1747.*

Moor, Nicholas, cordwainer, Penns Neck, will 9-1-1728, pr. 3-8-1728/9. Chd. John, Mary, Samuel.‡

Moses. Wf. Elizabeth, bap. 4-15-1744.*

Moore, Edward, m Martha Thompson, 11-10-1746.¶

Thomas, m Jean Tuff, 4-15-1730.¶

Moorehouse, Jonathan, Fairfield, inv. 3-16-4702/3. Son Jonathan.§

Morgan, Samuel, m Elizabeth Davis, 9-10-1731.¶

Morris, David, Elsenburgh, will 26th of 11th mo. (January), 1733/4. affirmed 2-16-1733. Wf. Jane; chd David, John Jeffreys (both under age), and Jane; bro. Lewis Morris.‡

David. Wf. Jane; s Joshua, b 10-3-1723.†

Grace, Elsenburgh, will 12-16-1748, affirmed 4-25-1749. Sisters Sarah Goodwin, Mary Goodwin, Jane Wright, Gaile, Ann and Rebecca Morris; bros.-in-law William and Thomas Goodwin; cousin (?nephew) John (under age), s of William Goodwin.‡

Joseph, int 4-16-1743. Wf. Prudence.§

Lewis, Elsinburgh, will 4th of 11th mo. (Jan'), 1739, affirmed 7-18-1749. Wf Grace; chd. Sarah, Mary, Grace, Jane, Jayl, Ann, Rebeckah; bro. David Morris, who has s David.‡

Redroe s of Lewis, b in Wales abt 1658, d in 1701. His wid m John Hart of Salem, in 1703.‖

Rothrak (Rudra). Wf. Jael; chd. David, b 12-8-1697/8; Joshua, b 5-14-1700; Jane, b 4-4-1702.†

Rothro, Elsinburgh, will 1-20-1702/3, pr. 9-24-1704 Wf. Jael; chd Jonathan, Joseph, Joshua, Lewis, David, Sarah and Jane (last 2 under age.‡

Rudra, s of Lewis, b in Pembrokeshire abt. 1658. Removed to Pennsylvania, ar. Philadelphia 1683; later came to Salem; thence to Elsinburgh; m Jael, dau. Richard Batty, b at Humford, Yorkshire, 1653. Jael re. to Pennsylvania in "Shield of Stockton," 3-8-1686, ar. Newcastle 5th mo.following. Chd. b at Elsinburgh, Jonathan, 12-16-1690; Joseph, b 6-3 1692; Sarah, b 12-16-1693; Lewis, b 11-23-1795/6.

Moslander, Johannes, int. 4-18-1734. Sarah Moslander, adm.‡

Moss, Abraham. Wf. Rebeckah; chd. Richard, b 11-6-1724/5; Isaac, b 11-18-1726/7; Hannah, b 10-1-1730; Thomas, b 11-22-1732/3.†

Richard. Wf. Rebeckah; s Abraham, b 12-14-1744/5.†

Muckleworth, William, pedler, int. 12-8-1747.§

Mufford, William, south side of Cohansey, will 7-28-1719. Wf. Mary; chd. Moses, Aaron, William, Benjamin, Stephen, Jonathan, Ephraim, Jacob, and Abigail Tomson.‡

Mulford, Aaron, Hopewell, will 11-29-1750, pr. 2-16-1750/51. Wf. Christian; chd. Moses, Mary, Daniel, Benjamin, William (last 3 under age).‡

Benjamin, late of New England, now of Munmouth River, weaver, will 11-28-1700, rec. 12-28-1700. Bro. Isaac Mullford; bros.-in-law Hugh Chard and James Mason §

Murdock (Murdagh), **John**, bricklayer, Mannington Precinct, will 12-25-1723, pr. 3-15-1724. Wf. Anne; chd. William, Margaret, and a dau. not named. ‡

Narthel, Christian, m Margaret Shoot, 6-30-1748.*

Nealson, Issarell, husb., Penns Neck, inv. 3-20-1799/1700. His wid. m Lucas Peterson. §

Neally, Joseph, Cohansey, m Elizabeth Booth, 8-16-1744.*

Neelson (Nellson, Nelison), **Mathias,** planter, Bowte Town, will 10-14-1673, rec. 4-12-1687. Wf. Annake Mathiason; Chd. Mathias and Israel Mathiason. ‡

Nelson, Anthony, m Phebe Elwell, 1-11-1748.*

Nevill, James, will 7-5-1688. Wf. Prudence; nephew Joseph Wyeth; neice Hannah Wyeth; bro. John Beard.§ and ‡

Newcomb, Joseph, int. 1-4-1733. Wf. Joyce. ‡

Newkirk, Cornelius, int. 10-20-1744. Wf. Rachel. ‡

Nicholdson, Samuel, Munmouth River. Adm. granted 6-12-1685. Wf. Ann. ‡

Nichols, John, m Ann Deaton, 12-28-1742.*
Thomas. Chd. David and Christiana, both bap. 9-13-1743.*
William, m Lucretia Widdish, 12-28-1742.*

Nicholson, Abel, Elsinborough, s of Samuel and Ann, m Mary, dau of William and Joanna Tyler. She was b in England in 1677. ‖
Abel. Wf. Mary; chd. Sarah, b 11-19-1694/5; Rachel, b 7-7.1698; Abel, b 1-13-1700/1; Joseph, b 12-4-1701; William, b 9-15-1703; Mary, b 11-1-1705; Ann, b 11-15-1707; John, b 5-8-1710; Ruth, b 9-9-1713; Samuel, b 12 10-1716/17; John, b 3-3-1719 †

Anne, wid., Alloways Creek, will 1st of 6th mo. (Aug.) 1693, rec. 6-30-1694. Chd. Samuel, Joseph, Abell, and Elizabeth Abbott, who has chd. Rachel, Mary and Elizabeth. §

Samuel, Alloways Creek, will 24th of 8th mo. (Oct.), 1694. Bros. Abell and Joseph; sister Elizabeth Abbot, who has chd Rachel, Mary, and Elizabeth. §

Samuel, Dunster, Co. Nottingham, Eng. Wf. Ann; chd. Rachel, b 2-7-1659; Elizabeth, b 3-22-1664; Samuel, b 2-30-1666; Joseph, b 2-30. 1669; Abel, b 5-2-1672. Came on "Griffith," ar. 9-23-1675. †

Samuel, m Sarah Dennis (both of Elsinboro), 1-23-1742/3. Chd. Abel, b 6-24-1744; Grace, b 9-11-1746; Abel, 6-16-1749; Rachel, b 10-1-1750; Abel, b 3-8-1752; Samuel, b 8-26-1753.†

William s of Abel and Mary Nicholson. Chd. Rachel, Ruth and William.‖

Nickson, James, husb., Mannington Precinct. Adm. granted 6-18-1702. Wf. Elizabeth.§

Jeremiah, Joneses Island, Cohansey, inv. 4-20-1727. Hannah Nickson, adm.‡

John, Salem Creek, husb.. will 28th of 2d mo. (Apr.) 1692, rec. 5-30-1692. Chd. James, Thomas, Jeremiah, Mary, Jane, Margery and Elizabeth; bro. Andrew Thompson.§

Nieukirk. Abraham, m Ann Richman, 12-23-1745. Chd. Elizabeth. bap. 11-15-1747; Rebekah, bap. 6-17-1749-50.*

Cornelius. Wf. Rachel; Dau. Sarah, bap 4-25-1741·2.*

Nix, Edward, m Mary Dickey, 12-7-1728.¶

Norton, John, Esq., int. 4-10;1735.‡

Nossiter, Thomas, Penns Neck. Adm. granted 8-12-1696. Wf. Ann.§

Oakford. Charles, emig. 1698. Chd. Elizabeth, b at Alloways Creek, 17th of 3d mo., 1698; Charles and Mary, twins, b 20th of 1st mo., 1701; John, b 12th of 1st mo., 1704. He married second, Margaret Denn, dau. of James and Elizabeth (Maddox) Denn. Chd. Mary and Susanna.‖

Charles, Alloways Creek, d 4-8-1711. Wf. Margrett; chd. Charles. John, Elizabeth, Mary, Susnnah (all under age).**

Charles. Wf. Mary; chd. Elizabeth, John, Charles and Mary, twins.†

Charles. Wf. Margaret, dau. of Isaac Smart; chd. Mary. b 1-21-1706.†

Charles. Wf. Easter, Esther or Hester; chd. Elizabeth, b 1-12-1727, Easter, b 12-22-1729/30; Charles. b 1-17-1731; Elizabeth, b 2-11-1736; James, b 8-2-1738; Margaret, b 11-3 (or 30)-1740/1.†

Charles, int. 7-14-1742 Wf. Esther.‡

John, m Rebecca Pittman, 10-2-1732.¶

John, Alloways Creek, m Hannah, dau. of George Coltson, 3-30-1733.†

John. Wf. Rebecka; chd. Samuel, b 7-4-1733; Mabel, b 6-13-1735; Sarah, b 12-21-1737/8; Rebeckah, b 8-17-1741; Susannah. b 2-2-1745.†

John. Wf. Hannah; chd. John, b 7-4-1734; Amos, b 2-2-1738, d 10-27-1765; Elizabeth. b 7-16-1741 †

Margrett, wid. of Charles, will 4-21-1711, pr. 5-18-1711. Chd. Mary, Susannah, Ann; sons-in-law (stepsons) Charles and John Oakford; dau.-in-law (stepdau.) Elizabeth Oakford; bro.-in-law Wade Samuel Oakford.**

Ogden, John. Wf. Hannah; s Richard, bap. 1-25-1740 1.*

John, Cohansey, will 12-21-1745; pr. 3-26-1746. Wf. Sarah; chd. John, Daniel, David, Thomas, Joseph, Mary, Samuel, dec'd; Jonathan, dec'd; and Sarah, dec'd.‡

Jonathan, weaver, Cohansey, will 2-10-1735; pr. 3-27-1736. Dau. Abigail, b 4-23-1733; mother-in-law Sarah Bishop.‡

Jonathan, Deerfield, will 11-21-1743, pr. 11-12-1745. Wf. Hannah; chd. Richard and Jonathan (both under age).‡

Richard, blacksmith, Fairfield, will 4-11-1726, pr. 5-26-1726. Wf. Elizabeth; dau Elizabeth.‡

Samuel; Deerfield, will 12-25-1742, pr. 1-26-1742 3. Wf. Mary; chd. Samuel, Malachia and Lorain.‡

O'Niel, Charles, clerk, adm. granted 11-18-1748.‡

Padgett, James, ward, son of Francis Padgett, Stowe Twp., 7-12-1749.***

Page, Anthony, Alloways Creek, inv. 7th of 12th mo. (Feb.), 1690 1. Wf. Mary.§

Anthony, planter, Cohansey, will 3-17-1712,13, pr. 4-30-1713. Mother Mary Shephard; bros. John Page and Samuel Shephard **

John, Stow, will 1-26-1713 14. pr. 4-20-1744. Wf. Patience; dau. Mary (under age); mother Mary Shepherd; wife's sons William and Samuel; cousin Samuel Stubens.‡

John. Wf. Rebecca; chd. Sarah, b 10-14-1745; James, b 11-3-1747; Mary, b 11-14-1749; Rachel, b 2-7-1752; Rebeckah, b 8-3-1754; John, b 8-4-1760.+

Paget, Andrew, m Elizabeth Craford, 6-10 1727.¶

Pagett, Andrew, Cohansey, inv. 11-20-1728. Elizabeth Pagett, adm.**

Ann, wid., int. 3-6-1739. Son William Murdock.‡

Francis, Cohansey, will 4-17-1735, pr. 5-27-1735. Wf. Isabel; chd. Francis, Sarah and a son not named.‡

James, int. 12-17-1733.‡

John, husb., Alloways Creek Precinct, will 8-9-1739, pr. 12-5-1739. Wf. Ann; nephews John McKnight, Moses and James Padget; Abigail Shirgeon, dau. of his eldest bro.; John, s of his bro. Thomas.‡

Robert, Stow, will 4-28-1713, pr. 6-11-1714. Wf. Abigail; chd. James, John, Samuel, Francis, Andrew, Thomas, Dorothy.‡

Paine, John, Aluways Creek, will 9-20-1726. Cousin Richard Smith of Amblebury, who has daus.-in-law (?stepdaus.) Sarah and Rachel Dennis, and daus. Grace, wf. of Lewis Morris; Ann, wf. of Joseph Darkin; William, wf. of Sarah Burroughs (sic.); Mary, wf. of William Smith of Mannington; Martha, wf. of Gabril Wood of Mannington; Elizabeth, wf. of Hugh Clefton of Salem; Rebekah, wf. of John Mason of Ann's Grove; Mary and Grace.‡ and §

Parker, James, Greenwich Twp., int. 4-17-1749.‡

Partleson, Ellen, Fines Point, non. will 4-14-1682, rec. 4-10-1689. Bros. Erick and Stephen Yearians and Lause Hendrickson.§

Parvin, Ebenezer, m Phebe Russel of Deerfield, 7-2-1744.*

Jeremiah, Deerfield. Chd. Rebekah and Jeremiah, both bap. 5-17-1741.*

Thomas, weaver, Cohansey, will 1-5-1742, pr. 4-18-1744. Wf. Rebecca; chd. Josiah, Mathew, Jeremiah, Silas, Sarah, Elizabeth, wf. of Moses Moore; and Hannah, wf. of Thomas Sayres, Jr.‡

Paulson, Tobias, m Mary Long, 8-24-1748.*

Pearce, James, blacksmith, Cohansey, will 12-7-1694, rec. 1-7-1694/5. Chd. Richard, Hannah, James and Mary.§

Pearson, Elizabeth, wid.; Salem, will 5-5-1720, pr. 5-17-1720. Dau. Elizabeth (under 16); father Richard Johnson; bro. Robert Johnson.‡

Isaac, of ye Brothers Forest, inv. 4-29-1708. Eldest s Isaac.**
John, Salem, inv. 1-26-1719/20. Wf. Elizabeth.**

Peck, John, weaver, Cohansey, will 10-18-1745, pr. 5-1-1748. Wf. Rebecca; chd. Jeremiah, John, Joseph, Abigail, and Herbert; granddau. Mary Ware.‡

Pedrick, John, Penns Neck, will 2-12-1728/9, pr. 4-28-1729. Wf. Elizabeth; chd. Mikell, John, Joseph, Mary Hanbe, Sarah, William, Jeremiah, Jacob, Thomas and Samuel (last 5 under age).‡

Joseph, Green's Neck, will 8-30-1748, affirmed 12-8-1748. Bros. Jacob and Thomas Pedrick; cousin Thomas Pedrick.‡

Michel, m Elizabeth Harding, 8-25-1748.¶

Roger, came from St. Paul's Parish, Eng., in 1662 and located near Salem.††

Roger, Pedrick's Neck, will 3-14-1692. Wf. Rebecka; chd. John, Thomas, Michael, and Philipp.§

Thomas, cooper, Penns Neck, will 12-21-1718, pr. 5-21-1719. Wf. Elizabeth; chd. Thomas, Philipp, Robart, Benjamin and Mary; bro. John Pedrick.‡

Peeters (Peterson), **Lucas,** Lucas Poynt, will 10-25-1686, rec. 6-20-1687. Chd. Peeter, Lucas, Haunce, Gabrill, Christian, Elizabeth, and Margrett Lacroy.§

Peirson, Henry, Cohansey, will 7-10-1747, inv. 2-2-1747/8. Chd. Henry, Azal, William, John, Eli and Amy.‡

Fennington, Alice, wid., adm. granted 4-3-1733.‡

Penten, Philip, m Mary Hutchinson, both of Alloways Creek, 1-16-1749.¶

Penton, Burton, shoemaker, Elsinburg, will 11-9-1749, pr. 12-15-1749. Bros. Abner, Amos and Daniel.‡

William, Alloways Creek, will rec. 7-4-1692. Chd. William, Jeane, and other daus. not named.§

William, Alloways Creek, will 2-24-1733, pr. 6-25-1735. Chd. Abner, Burton, John, Amos, William, Daniel, Mary, Elizabeth, Sarah, Martha and Miriam.‡

Perdue, William, Alloways Creek, will 5-11-1728, pr. 5-28-1728.‡

Perkins, William, Alloways, will 4-19-1729, pr. 5-2-1729. Chd. Mary, wf. of James Vance: Mathew, Jane, Susanna, David, John and Ann.‡

Peterson, Charles, m Ann Kent, 3-18-1691.¶

Charles, husb., Salem, inv. 4-7-1697. Wf. Ann.§

Gabriel, husb., Pilesgrove, will 12-20-1728, pr. 2-5-1728/9. Wf. Cristena; chd. Lucas, Gabriel, Hans, Marget, Mary, Peter, Lorence, Anna, Abraham, Jonas Crestina.**

Gabriel, int. 11-11-1737. Wf. Elizabeth.‡

Hance, Pilesgrove will 11-2-1728, pr. 12-31-1728. Wf. Sarah; chd. Mary, Sarah, Gabriel, Hance, Christian, Ellin.‡

Henry, int. 11-2-1741. Wf. Mary.‡

Jonas, Penns Neck, inv. 4-14-1729.‡

Laurence. Penns Neck, adm. granted 1-21-1725/6.‡

Lucas, husb, Penns Neck, will Oct. 1728, pr. 7-13-1732. Wf. Geen; chd. Lucas, Jonas, Tobias and Mary.**

Lucas, m Catherine Peterson, 10-17-1745.¶

Peter, Sr., Morris River, will 9-18-1733, pr. 10-18-1735. Wf. Ann; chd. Peter, Henry, Aaron, Gabriel, John, Mathias, Modlena, Rebecca Scull, Christian and Elener.‡

William, m Elizabeth Hughes, 6-12-1746.

Petterson, Lawrence, Penns Neck, inv. 1-14-1725/6.**

Peter, Penns Neck, inv. 2-14-1728/9.**

Christian, wf. of Gabriel, int. 7-17-1731.§

Phillpot, John, Penns Neck, will 3-29-1748, pr. 4-23-1748. Wf. Christiana; chd. John, Earick and Abraham.‡

Nicholas, Penns Neck, will 4-12-1696, rec. 11-11-1696. Wf. Ann; William, eldest, 2 not named; father William GillJohnson; uncle Yelious GillJohnson.§

Pickman, Richard, blacksmith, Penns Neck, inv. 4-21-1701. Son Richard.§

Pierson, Ann, wid., Salem Town, will 6-4-1749, pr. 1749. Chd. Mary, Henry and John (all under age).‡

Asahel. Wf. Mary; chd. Zebulon, bap. 10-26-1746.*

Isaac, Salem, adm. granted 5-18-1708. Son Isaac.‡

John, clerk, Salem Town, will 10-9-1747, pr. 10-29-1747. Wf. Ann; chd. Coleman, Henry and Mary (all under age) ‡

Pile, Sarah, wf. of Thomas Pile, inv. 3-4-1683/4. Dau. Elizabeth.§

Thomas, "citizen and upholsterer" of London, located upon his purchase. One of his three daus., Elizabeth, m Judge William Hall.††

Thomas, New Salem, will 17th of 6th mo. (Aug.), 1695. Dau. Elizabeth Hall; son-in-law William Hall.§

Pine, Lazarus. Wf. Mary; dau. Margaret, bap 8-12-1744.*

Pirey, William, Alloways Creek, will 7-1-1740, pr. 9-6-1740. Wf. Margaret; chd. Rebeccah McKnight, James, who has dau. Mary (under age); and Samuel.‡

Pitman, Richard, adm. granted 2-9-1707/8. Wf. Gertrude.‡

Pittman, William, lab., Penns Neck, inv. 10-1-1720.**

Platts, Jonathan. Wf. Jane; chd. Elizabeth, b 6-11-1731; Thomas, b 6-16-1734; Jane, 12-22-1740/41.†

Jonathan, Stow Creek, will 12-12-1748. affirmed 2-18-1748/9. Wf Jean; chd. Thomas (under age), Jonas, and Mary Evans.

Pledger, John, ship carpenter in Eng., came with wf. Elizabeth and son Joseph, on the Griffith.††

John, Plymouth Eng. Wf. Elizabeth; s Joseph, b in England, 6-4-1662; ar. on "Griffith," 9-23-1675. Son John, b in West Jersey, 9-27-1680.†

John, will 10-17-1694, rec. 12-19-1694. Wf. Elizabeth; chd. Joseph and John.§

John, Esq., Mannington, will 12-30-1743, pr. 1-4-1743. Chd. Elizabeth Casperson, and Martha, wf. of Edmund Weatherby; son-in-law Joseph Siddons; grandchd. Joseph (under age), Sarah and Dorothy (under age) Pledger, and John, Joseph and Pledger Redstreicke.‡

John, Jr., Alloways Creek Twp., will 7-28-1743, pr. 10-10-1743. Wf. Mary; chd. Joseph, Sarah and Dorothy (all under age); father John Pledger.‡

Joseph, Maninton Precinct, will 7-1-1697, rec. 7-20-1597. Wf. Mary, who has dau. Sarah Hurley; bro. John Pledger.§

Plummer, John, m Athey Henry, 6-21-1743.*

Pope, William, m Mary Horsley, 11-24-1702.¶

William, cordwainer, Cohansey, will 5-26-1715, pr. 6-29-1715. Wf. Ruth.‡

Powell, Ann, formerly Ann Curtis, will 9-25-1716. Cousins George, Edward and Jona Trenchard.‡

Howel, Fairfield, will 8-13-1716, pr. 12-29-1716. Wf. Elizabeth; chd. John (under age), Martha, Sarah, Walter, Elizabeth, Seaborn Foy.‡

Jeremiah. Wf. Elizabeth; chd. Mary, b 2-12-1696; Elizabeth, b 6-21-1698; Jeremiah, b 3-18-1701.†

Jeremiah, carpenter, Monmouth River, inv. 14th of 10th mo. (Dec.), 1700. Wf. Elizabeth.§

Jeremiah. Wf. Jane; chd. Elizabeth, b 12-22-1736; Mary, b 11-13-1738; John, b 12-5-1740.†

Jeremiah, Alloways Creek, will 11th of 12th mo., 1743/4. Chd. John, Elizabeth, and Mary (all under age); cousin Mary Mason.‡

John. Wf. Sarah, b 11-20-1714; Sorah, b 12-5-1740.†

John, int. 5-3-1743.‡

Walter, int. 1-22-1745. Jemima Powell, adm.‡

Preston, Isaac, Fairfield Precinct, will 12-16-1748, pr. 2-27-1749. Wf. Elizabeth; chd. Levi, Isaac, William, John, Elizabeth, and Joseph‡

Levi, Cahansey, int. 7-31-1731. Wf. Mary.‡

Price, William, m Ann Crocker, 8-10-1686/7.¶

Provoe, George, cordwainer, Alloways Creek, non. will, 8-1-1688. Cousin, Jean Wilke of Marish St., Bristol; Eng.§

Purple, John, Morsis's River, will 8-8-1749, pr. 4-9-1750. Chd. Ponthenia Custolow, Marsey and Abyah Peterson, who has chd. Catherin and Purple Peterson.‡

Purviance, Samuel, Alloways Creek. Wf. Mary, chd. Joanna, bap. 5-10-1741; Susanna, bap. 3-30-1745/6; Margaret, bap. 4-24-1748; Andrew, bap. 11-12-1749.*

Pyle, Ephraim, Pyle Grove. Adm. granted 8-25-1685. Bro.-in-law William Hall.§

Quinton, Tobias, Alloways Creek, will 10-16-1700, rec. 1-29-1700/1. Wf. Elizabeth.§

Tobias, emig. from Eng. Son Edward, d 1756, m Temperance, dau. of Daniel Smith.‖

Raines, Robert, m Christian Chandler, 12-25-1729.¶
Robert, bricklayer, Mannington, int. 1-8-1747/8. Wf. Christian.‡

Ranton, Mathew, Elsinborough, will 11-5-1739, affirmed 12-10-1739. Bro. William Ranton, of Ireland; sister Jean Ranton, of Ireland; cousins Samuel and Sarah Morton.‡

Reath, Deborah, int. 3-15-1744/5.‡

Redman, William. Wf. Mary; s John, b 8-27-1693.†

Redknap, Benjamin, Salem, will 1st of 11th mo. (Jan.), 1698/9. Chd. Joseph, Sarah, Mary.§

Redstreak, John, Penns Neck, will 12-17-1737, pr. 1-10-1738. Wf. Elizabeth; chd. John, Joseph and Pledger; sister-in-law Mary Pledger; cousins Rebecca Johnson and Rachel Shivers.‡
John. ward, 16 yrs., s of John of Penns Neck, 7-18-1747.§

Reed, John, merchant, int. 8-28-1746.‡

Reeve, Joseph, s of Mark and Ann, m 1722, Ellinor Bagnall. Chd. Mark, b 28th of 12th mo., 1723; Joseph, b 5th of 7th mo., 1725, m Milicent, dau. of Joseph and Hannah Wade; John, b 5th of 1st mo., 1730, m Elizabeth, dau. of John and Ann Brick; Mary, and Benjamin.‖
Joseph, Cohansey, m Ellen Bagnall, Alloways Creek, 11-31-1722.§
Joseph, south side of Cohansey, will 11-11-1748, pr. 3-1-1748. Chd. Mark, Joseph, John, Samuel, Mary, and Benjamin (under age).‡
Mark, Cesariae River, will 10th of 9th mo. (November), 1694, rec 11-31-1694. Wf. Ann; chd. Charles, Marke and Joseph.§
Reeve, Mark, m Ann Hunt, 12-3-1686.¶

Reeves, David, Alloways Creek, will 11-14-1749, pr. 12-2-1749. Chd. David and Joshua; dau.-in-law Partheny Reeves; grandchd. Joshua Reeves, Mary, dau. of David Reeves, and Elizabeth, dau. of Joshua Reeves.‡

Remington, John, int. 2-15-1732/3. Wf. Sarah.‡
Sarah, wid, int. 3-28-1733.‡
William, m Mary Woodhouse, 4-13-1693.¶

Remmenton, William, Cohansey, inv. 4-4-1707. Wf. Mary.‡

Rice, Thomas. Wf. Mary; chd. Philip, b 1-16-1739/40; Hannah, b 5-10-1742; Griffith, b 2-26-1747; Sarah, b 8-20-1750; John, b 4-26-1753.†

Richard, Godfreed, m Catharine Garrison, 5-31-1748.*

Richardson, Edward, Cohansey. Wf. Jane; chd. Joseph and John, both bap. 7-29-1744.*

Richman, Herman, Pilesgrove, will 6-9-1744, affirmed 8-7-1744. Wf. Elizabeth; chd. Jacob, eldest son; Uldrick, Michael (under age), Margaret, eldest dau.; Mary, Ann, Elizabeth, Maudlen and Sarah.‡

John, m Sarah Vanmeter, 1-27-1741/2; chd. Rebekah, bap. 5-1-1743; Isaac, bap. 11-17-1745; Abraham, bap. 5-21-1749.*

Ridley, James, Salem Town, will 3-29-1705, pr. 3-16-1705/6. Wf. Rebeckah; chd. William, Mary and Rebeckah (all under age); bro.-in-law Thomas Berry, of Talbot Co., Md.‡

William. Wf. Sarah; chd. James, b 4-14-1716; Rebeckah, b 1-4-1718/19; William, b 5-1-1721.†

William, weaver, Salem, will 4-7-1726, pr. 8-19-1726. Chd. James, William and Rebeckah (all under age.‡

William, carpenter, Salem Town, int. 11-13-1749. Hannah Ridley, adm.§

William, ward, aged 18, 12-4-1739.§

Riley, Joseph, will 1-25-1734/5, pr. 2-24-1734/5. Wf. Rachel; chd. Aaron, Joseph, Mark, Elihu (all under age); bro.-in-law John Remington.‡

Robards (Roberts), **John,** inv. 10-4-1715.**

Roberts, Henry, Sr., inv. 12-13-1714. Mary Roberts, adm.**

Henry, Jr., will 11-9-1713, pr. 6-2-1714. Wf. Ann.‡

John, Alloways Creek, will 2-8-1729/30, pr. 2-14-1729/30.‡

Lemuel, Cohansey, inv. 3-22-1729/30. Deborah Roberts, adm.**

Samuel, 6-20-1730. Adm. granted Deborah Roberts.‡

Robeson, William, planter, 6-24-1689.§

Robins, Richard, Cohansey, will 21st of 3d mo., 1715, pr. 9-28-1715. Wf. Catherine; chd. Richard, Obediah, Lydia and Hope; son-in-law (?stepson) Nathaniel Bacon (under age).‡

Robert, Cohansey, will 1-11-1715/16, pr. 2-16-1715/16. Wf. Hannah; son Latten.‡

Robinson, James, Deerfield Twp., int. 4-17-1749.‡

John, Mannington, will 5-10-1734, pr. 7-13-1734. Wf. Kathrain; chd. Elizabeth, Kathrain, Jean, John, Margaret.‡

John, m Mary Thompson, 9-20-1743. Chd. William, bap. 2-16-1746/7; Euphan, bap. 7-9-1749.

Roch, John, Deerfield Twp., int. 11-13-1750.***

Rogers, Jonathan, m Bridget Conchton, 4-28-1745/6.¶

Rolfe, John, Esq., will 11-20-1742, pr. 12-9-1742. Chd. John, Josiah (under age), and Mary Rolfe of Newcastle, Pa.; son-in-law David Ross and Sarah his wf.‡

Rolph, James, came to Salem abt. 1700. Dau. Elizabeth m Thomas Clement. His wid. m Aaron Bradway.‖

Rose, James, Fairfield Precinct, will 6-14-1749, pr. 12-20-1749. Wf. Elizabeth; chd. Abigail Hays, James, Hannah and Elizabeth; cousin Thomas Harris.‡

John. Wf. Mary; chd. Elizabeth, bap. 8-10-1740; Abigail, bap. 8-22-1742.*

John. Wf. Elizabeth; chd. Ezekiel, bap. 6-9-1745.*

Rowland, Samuel, Grinwich, inv. 4-11-1728. Sarah Rowland, adm.‡

Royley, Joseph, will 4-13-1699, rec. 4-4-1700. Wf. Elizabeth; bros. James and Thomas Royley.§

Ruge, Benjamin, m Ann Craven, 3-20-1731.¶

Rugg, Benoni, Cohansey, int. 1-31-1736. Wf. Ann.‡
William, weaver, Cohansey, bond of adm. 10-28-1727.**

Rumsey, Daniel, Mannington, inv. 7-18-1718. Wf. Grace.‡
Elizabeth, wid. Robert, Salem Town, will 2-6-1713/14, pr. 6-23-1714. Bro. Rinier Van Hyst.‡
Robert, cordwainer, Salem Town, will 3-17-1712/13, pr. 5-4-1714. Wf. Elizabeth; dau. Ruth (under age).‡
William, cordwainer, Manneton, will 5th of 3d mo., 1702, pr. 9-27-1702. Wf. Ruth.

Rutherford, Allen, int. 3-26-1735.‡
James, int. 11-17-1744.‡

Ryle, James, Cohansey, will 4-23-1741, pr. 6-8-1743. Chd. James, John, Thomas, and Joseph.‡

Saley (Salley, Solbey), **Timothy,** Cohansey. Wf. Deborah recommends adm. 5-26-1726.**

Sallaway, Thomas, weaver, will 10-28-1689, rec. 4-28-1694. Dau. Margrett; bro. William Sallaway of Philadelphia.§

Salter, Henry, d at Salem 4-11-1679. Son John.§

Sagel, Ann, wid. Son Thomas, bap. 10-16-1746.*

Sanghurst, Edward, m Elisha (?) Crow 5-16-1733.¶

Sargent, Spencer, cururgen (surgeon), Salem, will 9-25-1713, pr. 11-2-1713. Father William Sargent of Youghall, Ire.§

Satterthwaite, Isaac, weaver, Salem Town, will 3-3-1734, pr. 12-18-1737. Wf. Phebe; chd. Isaac, Anne, Rebecca, Sarah and Margate (all under age).‡

Savage, Mary, wid., Mannington Precinct, will 1-9-1725/6, pr. 1-29-1725/6. Son Joseph Waddington (under age).**

Savoy, Abraham, Penns Neck, bond of adm. 6-20-1727. Wf. Mary.**

Isaac, Penns Neck, non. will 11-4-1694. Wf. Breeta; chd. David, Greta, Margrett, Abraham, Isaac, John.§

Sayers, Ebenezer, Cohansey, inv. 11-23-1725. Naomi Sayres. adm.‡

Sayre, David, Sr., Cohansey, will 2-16-1740/1, pr. 12-8-1744. Chd. David (eldest s) Job, Dorothy Pagett (eldest dau.), Hannah Plummer, Christian Mulford, Rebecca Gelaspse, and Anna Sayre; grandchild Mary Platts; son-in-law Thomas Pagett.‡

David, husb., Cohansey, will 2-21-1742, pr. 4-26-1742. Wf. Ruth; chd. David, Daniel, William, Thomas, James (unker age) Hannah Dayton, Eleanor, Ruth, Mary, Prudence (under age).‡

Elisha, Cohansey, will 4-12-1726, pr. 4-19-1726. Sister Tamsun Vance; cousins Joseph and Richard Sayer and Israel Pettey.‡

Ephraim, Cohansey, Lower Precinct, will 12-31-1715, pr. 1-24-1715/16. Wf. Sarah; chd. Ephraim, Patience, Sarah and Temperance.**

James, Stow Creek, b 1720, son of Thomas and Rachel. Chd. James, John and Ephraim Abbott Sayres.‖

Joseph, Cohansey, will 4-10-1710, pr. 4-19-1710. Wf. Presilah; chd. Joseph, Ebenezer, Elisha, Samuel, Tamson; bros. David and Ephraim Sayre.‡

Joseph, Lower Precinct, Cohansey, will 12-27-1715, pr. 1-24-1715/16. Wf. Margarett; chd. Joseph and Richard (both under age); sister Tamson Vaunce; father Joseph Sayre; uncle Ephraim Sayre.**

Richard, Salem, will 9-12-1736, affirmed 12-18-1738. Mother Ann Johnson; sister Mary, wf. of John Pledger, Jr.; bros. Joseph Sayre and Robert Johnson; cousins Richard, Thomas and Job Butcher, sons of uncle Richard Butcher of Stow Creek.‡

Thomas, s of Jonas. Wf. Rachel; chd. Thomas, James, Leonard, Lot, and Ruth, wf. of James Daniels.‖

Thomas, s of Thomas and Rachel Sayres, m Rachel Abbott in 1742. Chd. Abbott, b 1743; Reuben, Hannah, David, Reuel, Joseph, Dennis, Rachel, Thomas, Dorcas, and William.‖

Scogen, Johanas, husb., Penns Neck, will 12-17-1728, pr. 11-25-1729. Wf. Katthren; chd. John, Jonas, Jacobis and Mary.‡

Jonas, Penns Neck, will 12-13-1733, pr. 3-1-1733. Wf. Sarah; chd. Jonas and Mary (both under age); son-in-law (?stepson) William Vaniman (under age).‡

Scoggin, John, Penns Neck, non. will recorded 9-26-1692. Wf. Barbary; chd. 2 sons (under age) and 2 daus. not named.§

John, husb., Penns Neck, will 11-19-1694, rec. 7-10-1795. Wf. Elizabeth; chd. Jonas, Mathias, Johanes (all under age, and 2 daus not named.§

John, Jonas, Jacob, Mary and Elizabeth (last 3 under 14 yrs.), chd. of Johannes and Catherine, both dec'd, wards 1-1-1734.‡

Jonah, m Ann Hall, 2-25-1748.¶

Scole, James, husb., Salem, inv. Aug. 14th and 19th, 1690. Bro. John Scole.§

John, cordwainer, will 6th of 8th mo. (Oct.) 1700. Dau. Edith.§

Scott, Timothy, int. 2-24-1747/8. Sarah Scott, adm.

Seagrave, William, Jr., Deerfield Twp., int. 6-24-1749. Aribela Seagrave, adm.***

Sedden (Sidded, Sydden), **Henry,** blacksmith, Salem, inv. 12-14-1725. Wf. Hannah.**

Seeley, David, m Mary Richman, 12-18-1745. Chd. Deborah, bap. 5-31-1747; Benjamin, bap. 5-6-1750.*

Henry. Wf. Mary; chd. Henry, bap. 11-20-1743; Hannah, bap. 10-13-1745.*

John, int. 6-26-1733.‡

John, int. 9-17-1750.***

Seelye (Selcy), **Ephraim,** miller, Fairfield, will 3-9-1722,3, pr. 4-10-1723. Wf. Mary; chd. Ephraim, Elizabeth, Sarah and Phebe.‡

Seelee (Selcy, Seely), **Benjamin,** carpenter, Cohansey, adm. granted 3-20-1721/2.¶

Seneca, Anders, came from Sweden. Chd. Broor and Anders.‖

Anders, Jr. Chd. Sinick, m 1718, Margaret Wigorvie; John, m Ann GillJohnson.‖

Sinick, s of Anders Seneca, Jr., m 21st of 9th mo., 1718, Margaret Wigorvie. Chd. Andrew, Sarah, Anna, and a dau. not named,‖

Seyars, Joseph, Cohansey, adm. granted 7-20-1716. Wf. Margret.‡

Sharp, Isaac, emig. from Ireland abt. 1730 and settled at Blessington, now Sharptown. Was Judge of Court of Salem county in 1741. Chd. Anthony and Edward.††

Isaac, emig Chd. Samuel, Edward, Anthony, Mary, Jaiel, Hannah D., Sarah, Rachel Wyncoop, and Elizabeth.‖

Isaac. Wf. Elizabeth; chd. Mary, b 6-2-1744; Hannah, b 7-8-1746; Sarah, b 9-9-1750; Anthony, b 11-3-1752; Rachel, b 12-27-1754; Samuel, b 5-4-1756; Margaret, b 8-21-1758.†

Joseph, bro. of Isaac, prob. came with Isaac; res. at Sharptown. Chd. Isaac and Joseph.††

Shaw, Benjamin, (called Edmund in Jurat of admx.) Bond of adm. 11-18-1705. Wf. Sarah.**

Carll, Fairfield Precinct, will 3-26-1750, pr. 4-21-1750. 1st wf., Hannah; 2d wf. Elizabeth; chd. Carll (firstborn, by Hannah), Ryal, Hannah and Mary; bro. Joshua Shaw.‡

Edmund, adm. granted 3-18-1705-6. Wf. Sarah.‡

Edmund, Sr., Fairfield, will 3-13-1718/19, pr. 12-20-1719. Wf Rachel; chd. Edmund, Nathan, Richard, Carell, Joshua, Hezekiah, and 4 daus. not named; bro. Abiel Carell.‡

Hezekiah, m Hannah Buck, 1-1-1746.*

Nathan, Deerfield. Wf. Mary; chd. Nathan, Mary, John, Zachariah, Sarah, Ephraim, Anna, all bap. 8-31-1740; Annanias, bap. 6-20-1742.*

Sheepherd, David, will 11-20-1695, rec. 4-4-1696. Wf. Eve; chd. David, John, Joseph, Ruth Abbott, Eve, Elizabeth and Hannah.§

Shehaiel, Martinus, Penns Neck, inv. 11-12-1694. Albert Hendricks, father of the wid.§

Sheiahel, Haunce, planter, Penns Neck, non. will 9-1-1689, pr. 5-2-1692. Wf. Margrett; s Martinus.§

Shephard, John, Cohansey, husb., will 1-9-1715, pr. 2-24-1715/16. Bros. Joseph, David and Enoch; sisters Hannah Gilman, who has son David; Eve and Elizabeth Shephard.‡

Shepherd, Daniel, Cohansey, will 1-20-1734/5, pr. 4-26-1735. Wf. Deborah; dau. Sarah; bro Thomas Shepherd.‡

Dickason, will 3-11-1742/3, pr. 11-28-1749. Wf. Eve; chd. Stephen, Patience, wf. of William Paulin, Dickenson, John, Jonadab, Ann and Eve.‡

Edward, Mannington, int. 2-26-1749.‡

Enoch, husb., Cohansey, will 10-3-1717, pr. 9-23-1718. Wf. Elizabeth; chd. Daniel, Sarah, Enoch, John, Thomas and Elizabeth (all under age); bro. Job Shepherd.‡

Eve, wid. of David Shepherd, inv. 10-13-1710. Son David.§

Eve, Cohansey, wid. of Dickason Shepherd, will 2-3-1749/50, pr. 3-12-1749/50. Chd. Stephen, Dickason, John, Jonadab, Eve Sakel, Ann and Pesians.‡

James, Cesariae River, non. will 1690, rec. 5-8-1691. Chd. Hester and Rachel.§

James, Cohansey, will 7-7-1713. pr. 11-13-1713. Wf. Anna, dau. of John Chatfield; wife's dau., Mary Hodge (?); bros. Moses and David Shepherd.**

John, Cohansey, Bond of adm. 10-6-1710. Son Dickeson Shepherd.‡

Joseph, Cohansey, will 2-6-1723, pr. 12-24-1728. Wf. Ann; chd. Jonathan (under age), Lucey, Ann, Hannah (under age); cousin David Gilman (under age).**

Mary, wid., Cohansie, will 1-11-1713/14, pr. 4-20-1714. Sons John Page and Samuel Shepherd.‡

Thomas, Cohansey, will 6-17-1747, pr. 7-29-1747. Wf. Rachel; chd. John. Mary (both under age), and Daniel.‡

Sheppard, Abel, b 1730, s of David and Anna Sheppard, m Abigail, dau. of Caleb Barrett. He d 4-13-1773; his wf d 3-8-1806. Chd. Phoebe, Abel, Caleb, Abigail, Dickinson, Anna, James, Rebecca, David and Sarah.††

David. Wf. Anna, prob. dau. of Dickinson Sheppard; chd. David, Abel, Phebe, Thomas and Lucy.††

John, settled in Back Neck, Fairfield, in 1683, and d in 1710. Chd. Dickinson, Enoch and Job.††

Shere, Margrett, wid, Penns Neck, non. will rec. 4-16-1695. Son Mortah (other chd. not named).§

Sherry, Samuel. Wf. Mary; chd. Samuel, Sarah, Recompence, all bap. 8-17-1740, Priscilla, bap. 4-15-1744, Mary, bap. 4-6-1746; Phebe, bap. 5-22-1748.*

Shields, William, carpenter, Salem Town, int. 5-16-1741. Wf. Rachel.§

Shiwin, James, bond of adm. 5-2-1717.—*Administration Bonds, 1716-1756.*

Short, William, Cohansey, d 11-2-1715. Wf. Elinor.‡

Shroverde, Cornelius, came from Holland in 1684.††

Shugers, John, clothier, Penns Neck, bond of adm. 9-7-1720 Sarah, his wid., m Robert Cammell.**

Shute, Francis, Penns Neck, inv. 8-23-1700. Wf. Christian.§

Siddon, Henry, blacksmith, Salem. Bond of Hannah Siddon adm., 12-22-1725.‡

John, Deerfield Twp., int. 10-9-1749.***

William. Wf. Hannah; chd. Hannah, b 9-1-1732; Sarah, b 5-24-1735; Jane, b 4-1-1738; Deborah, b 11-30-1739/40; William, b 11-16-1742/3; Ezekiel, b 7-10-1745; Elizabeth, b 10-20-1747; Edward, of Mannington, b 5-25-1750; Isaac. b 11-13-1754.†

Silver, Archibald, husb., Mannenton Creek, inv. 6-14-1703.§

Simrell, William. Wf. Mary; chd. Sarah, bap. 9-2-1744; John, bap. 8-24-1746; Margaret, bap. 3-14-1747/8; William, bap. 11-18-1749/50.*

Sims, John, int. 8-27-1743. Wf. Sarah.‡
Samuel, m Lydia Willis, of Alloways Creek, 12-10-1747.¶

Sineker, Andrew, Penns Neck, will 7-17-1696, rec. 4-11-1700 Wf. Sarah; chd. Johanss, Engrey, Andrew, "son by this wf."§

Siniker, Johannas, husb., Piles Grove, will 12-18-1729, pr. 5-26-1735. Wf. Gartrow; chd. Stephen, Susannah, Isaac, Andrew and Bridget.‡

Sinnick, John, Penns Neck, will 11-3-1739, pr. 12-1-1739. Wf. Ann; chd. John Sarah and Sinnick Sinnickson; bro. Sinnick Sinnickson.‡

Sinnickson, Penns Neck, will 6-23-1750, pr. 7-28-1750. Wf. Mary; chd. Andrew, Sarah (under age), and Ann, wf. of Peter Peterson.‡

Sirredge, John, planter, Cohansey, inv. 1-26-1687/8. Bro. William Sirredge.§

William; bricklayer, Salem Town, inv. 5-3-1706 **

Skeere (Scear), **Hance,** Penns Neck, will 12-18-1717, pr. 9-2-1723. Wf. Anne (endorsed Elizabeth in bond of adm.) m ——— Demire; chd. Marten, Mary, Kaetern, Erick, and 3 daus not named; bro. Laurance Skeare.‡

Skeen, Jonas, Cesariae River, inv. 3-2-1694/5. Wf. Katherine §
Jonas, Penns Neck, int. 1-2-1748.‡

Skønner, William, husb., Mannington Precinct, will 12-15-1732, pr. 12-25-1732 ‡

Sluby, Henry, inv. 3-9-1712/13.**

Smart, Isaac, b at Greatleton., Eng., in 1658, s of Roger; came on Griffith, ar. 9-23-1675; m Elizabeth, dau. Andrew and Isabelle Thompson, 2-26-1683. Chd. Isaac, b Middle Neck, near Salem, 7-21 or 7-22-1684; Mary, b 10-21-1685; Nathan, b 5-8-1692; Rebeckah, b 12-23-1695/6; Ann, b 6-20-1697; Isabel, b 9-16-1699.†

Isaac, emig., d in 1700. His wid., Elizabeth. in 1701, m Edward Keasbey.‖

Isaac, Middle Neck, will 3d of 8th mo. (Oct.), 1700. Wf. Elizabeth; chd. Nathaniel (under age), Mary, Sarah, Hannah, Rebeckah.§

Nathan, planter, Middle Neck, near Elsenburg. Adm. granted bro. Isaac Smart, 11-22-1681.§

Nathan. Wf. Deborah; chd. Mary, b 5-22-1714; Elizabeth, b 1-4-1715; Hannah, b 12-23-1717/18; Isaac, b 4-15-1721 (2-4-1721 O. S.); Edward, b 5-14-1724.†

Smith, Alexander, m Hannah Ashbury, 8-8-1687.¶

David, Smithfield, will 12-3-1694, pr. 2-2-1694/5. Dau. Sarah (under age); bros. Jonathan, Jeremiah and Daniel Smith.§

David. Wf. Mary; chd. Sarah, b. 11-17-1701.†

David, cooper, Salem. int. 4-3-1731. Sarah Smith, adm.§

Daniel. Wf. Dorcas; chd. Martha, b 11-17-1701; Dorcas, b 7-27-1703; Daniel, b 10-16-1705.†

Daniel, Aloes Creek, Smithfield or Munmouth River, will 9-3-1714, pr. 1-16-1716/17, Son Daniel (under age); cousins Samuel Smith, Jr., and Thomas Craven; bros. Samuel and Jere Smith.‡

Daniel, carpenter, Manington, will 1-5-1747, pr. 2-24-1748/9. Wf. Elizabeth; Chd. Seath, Anne, Solomon, John, Daniel, Benjamin (all under age).‡

Eleazar Wf. Mary; chd. Martha and Rebecca, both bap. 8-10-1740; Rebekah, bap. 11-15-1741; Eliazer, bap. 4-22-1744; Elizabeth, bap. 5-29-1746; Sarah, bap. 6.23-1748 *

Giles, b 18th of 2d mo., 1719, s of Samuel Smith of Mannington, m Rebecca, dau. of Samuel F. Hedge. Son Christopher.‖

Jeremiah, will 11-24-1734, pr. 10-9-1735. Wf. Sarah; chd. Jeremiah, Job (under age), Sarah, Elizabeth and Mary.‡

John, s of John, b at Disson, Co. Norfolk; Eng., 7-20-1623, m Martha, dau. of Christopher Crafts; ar. in Griffith, 9-23-1675, with 4 chd., Daniel, b at Worksay, Nottinghamshire, 12-10-1660, Samuel, b 3-10, or 3-18-1664; David, b 12-4-1671; Sarah b Parish of Pauls Shadwell, London, 12-4-1671; Jonathan, b at New Salem, 10-27-1675; Jeremiah, b 9-14-167—.†

John, s of William, b abt. 1645, in 1683, m Susannah, dau. of Edward Marcy, and re. with wf., 2 chd. and manservant John Hogben, in ship Charles, ar. at Newcastle and settled at Salem. Chd. Susannah, b 8-8-

1687; John, b at Krindaill Hill, in 1689; which said John the younger settled in Mannington.†

John, weaver, Amwelbury, will 1-20-1690 1, rec. 5-4-1691. Chd. John, Thomas, Elizabeth, Letisia, dau. Walker, "my son John Bacon;" bro. John Bacon.§

John, weaver, Amwelbury, will 11-5-1694, rec. 2-12-1695/6. Wf. Sarah; chd. John and Richard (both under age).§

John. Wf. Susannah; chd. Elizabeth, b 3-3-1703.†

John. Wf. Hannah; chd. John, b 12-26-1712.†

John, Ambleberry, bond of adm. 1-27-1715/16.‡

John. Wf. Sarah; chd. Samuel, b 12-6-1719.†

John, cordwainer, Salem Town, inv. 5-23-1721.

John, Hedgefield, will 14th of 12th mo. (Feb.) 1721/2, pr. 8-27-1728. Wf. Susannah; chd. John, Joseph, William, Elizabeth, Sarah Goodwin and Mary; grandchd. John, Samuel, Elizabeth and Thomas Smith, and John and Elizabeth White.‡

John. Wf. Sarah; chd Richard, b 11-10-1743/4; Hill, b 4-15-1745, d 8-15-1801; John, b 11-27-1748/9†

John, Alloways Creek, will 3-23-1743, pr. 5-1-1744. Wf. Mary; chd. Samuel, Mary, Ann, Margaret, Jean and Hannah (the latter unnamed yet); cousin Daniel Smith of Alloways Creek.‡

John, Amwelberry, will 7-17-1749, affirmed 8-19-1749. Wf. Sarah; chd. Richard, Hill and John (all under age); bro. Richard Smith.‡

John. Wf. Mary; chd. Samuel and Hannah, bap. 6-26-1746.*

Jonathan, Alloways Creek, will 4-2-1723, pr. 5-7-1726. Wf. Mary chd. Jonathan, Jaemes, Isaac, Elizabeth, Condon, Eadeth, Martha and Deburah ‡

Joseph, s of John and Susannah. Son Thomas, m in 1740, Sarah, d Elisha and Abigail Bassett of Pilesgrove.‖

Mathew, inv. 3-10-1711/12.**

Pile, m Rebecca Hedge, 11-4-1745.¶

Richard, Elsinborough, will Feb. 1740, pr. 3-11-1740. Chd. John, Richard (13 yrs. old), Rachel, Sarah Dennis, Merriman, Mary, and Grace.‡

Robert, Elsenburgh, laborer, will 9th of 3d mo. (May), 1721; inv. 5th of 4th mo. (June), 1721. Bros. Thomas and Richard Smith; sisters Elizabeth and Mary Smith.**

Samuel. Wf Hannah; chd. Piles, b 10-18-1719; Mary, b 8-26-1721; Elizabeth, b 7-1-1726; Mary Ann, b 2-23-1729.†

Samuel, Mannington, will 5th of 10th mo. (Dec.), 1737, affirmed 12-27-1737. Wf. Hannah; chd. Pile, Hannah, Elizabeth and Mary Ann.‡

Solomon, Greenwich Township, int. 3-14-1748.***

Thomas, Cohansey, will 11-22-1692, rec. 6-25-1692. Wf. Ann, m Thomas Yard. Chd. Sollomon, Seth, Jeremyah, Deborah (all under age).§

Thomas, Amwelbury, inv. 5th of 10th mo. (Dec.), 1694. Wf. Mary; mother Widow Mary Smith.§

Thomas, Mannington Precinct, will 3-14-1732/3, affirmed 7-17-1733. Wf. Grace; chd. Mary and Grace (both under age); son-in-law Daniel Rumsey; dau.-in-law Ruth Rumsey; bro. William Smith.‡

Thomas, of Mannington, m Sarah Bassett, of Pilesgrove, 2-3-1740. Chd. William, b 8-31-1741; David, b 7-17-1744; Thomas b 4-28-1747.†

William, int. 2-26-1739. Wf. Mary.‡

William, Mannington, int., 7-8-1740. Wf. Mary.‡

Sneathen, Jeremiah, Alloways Creek, m Elizabeth Hogben, 6-13-1747.¶

Snooke, John, tailor, Salem, inv. 3-29-1693. Wf. Hannah.§

Solley, Timothy, will 4-1-1743. Bro. Nathan Solley.‡

Songhurst, Editha, wid., Salem Town, will 12-4-1734, pr. 2-10-1735. Chd. Mary, George and William Crow.‡

Edward, int. 1-21-1733. Wf. Editha.‡

Souther, Charles. Son Jacob, bap. 9-24-1749.*

Peter, weaver, Penns Neck, will 12-21-1748, pr. 12-10-1750. Wf. Margaret; chd. John, William, Phillips, Charles and Katherine.§

William, m Catherine Pawlson, 6-10-1745.*

Standbank (Stanbank), **John,** Penns Neck, inv. 1-18-1719/20.‡ and §

Standford, Thomas, rope maker, will 11-26-1722, pr. 1-8-1722/3. Wf. Miriam; chd. Joan, wf. of John Mahu, who has s John; Anne, wf. of Benjamin Jones, who has chd. Rachel, Lydia, John, Jerusha, Benjamin and Standford Jones ‡

Miriam, Cohawkin, Pilesgrove Precinct, wid. of Thomas, will 1-8-1722/3, pr. 1-19-1722/3. Chd. Miriam, wf. of Thomas Smith, tailor; Mary, wf. of Randle Huitt; granddau. Rachel Elwell; sons-in-law Henry and William Paullin.‡

Stanley, Onesiphorus, husb., Penns Neck, inv. 2-4-1697/8.§

Stathem, Philipp, Cohansey, will 11-21-1716, pr. 3-18-1717. Wf. Mary; chd. Philipp, Hugh, Ruth, Jeane, Mary and Margaret (all under age).‡

Philipp, yeo., bond of adm. 5-17-1729.‡

Thomas, yeo., Cohansey, inv. 11-27-1696. Wf. Ruth.§

Thomas, Jr., Cohansey, will 11-17-1744, pr. 1-20-1743/5. Wf.

Keziah; father Thomas Stathem; bro. Jonathan Stathem.‡

Thomas, Cumb. Co., will 4-12-1749, pr. 10-2-1749. Wf. Mary; dau. Catherine ‡

Zebulon, yeo., Cohansey Precinct, will 9-27-1716, pr. 4-5-1721. Wf. Marcy; bros. Philipp and Thomas.‡

Stethems, Mary, int. 42-1-1735.‡

Stewart, John, m Mary Wade, both of Alloways Creek, 11-1-1734. Chd. Elizabeth, b 9-27-1735; Lidya, b 12-16-1737; Samuel, b 12-26-1740; John, b 7-16-1743; Mary, b 1-6-1746; Ann, b 11-14-1748; James, b 3-26-1751; Milisent, b 6-8-1754; Joseph, b 4-1-1758.†

Stonebank, Thomas, Pilesgrove, will 4-26-1749, pr. 2-13-1750. Wf. Mary; s John.§

Thomas Wf. Mary; chd. John, Thomas, Richard, James, William, Joseph and Mary, all bap. 7-31-1743; Elizabeth, bap. 4-21-1745; Samuel, bap. 10-4-1747.*

Stowe, Jane, wid., Mannington Precinct, will 12th of 1st mo. (Feb.), 1736/7. Chd. Thomas, John, Mary, Elizabeth, Joanna and Jane.‡

Thomas, int. 1-9-1735. Wf. Jane.‡

Thomas, int. 12-10-1747. Wf. Sarah ‡

Stratton, Benjamin, Cohansey, inv. 9-27-1716. Mary Stratton, adm ‡

Straughan (Straghan), **David,** Penns Neck, will 11-13-1721, pr. 11-25-1721. Chd. David, Addam, John, and Elizabeth Perkins.**

David, int. 1-23-1735. Wf. Hannah.‡

Street, William, int. 2-28-1739.‡

Stretch, Bradway, b 1724, s of Joseph and Hannah Stretch, m Sarah, b 15th of 11th mo., 1701, dau. of John and Mary (Chambless) Hancock. Chd. Hannah, b 6th of 2d mo., 1725, m Wade Barker; William, David, James, Sarah, Mary, Bradway and Eleanor.‖

Bradway, Alloways Creek, will 28th of 10th mo. (Dec.) 1748, affirmed 5-11-1749. Wf. Mary; chd. John, David, James, William, Sarah, Mary, Eleanor.‡

Daniel, Alloways Creek Precinct, will 3-19-1735, pr. 5-1-1735. Wf. Elizabeth; chd. Isaac, Daniel, Martha, Hannah, Mary and Sarah; father Peter Stretch.‡

Joseph. Wf. Hannah; chd. Bradway, b 3-11-1702; Joseph, b 1-16-1704, d 1-1-1767.†

Joseph, emig. from England abt. 1695, m Hannah, b in Salem, 7-7-

1681, dau. of Edward and Mary Bradway. Chd. Bradway and Joseph.‖

Joseph, m Deborah Smith, 3-9-1727.¶

Joseph. Wf. Deborah. Chd. Mary, b 5-2-1728; Joseph, b 9-3-1732, d 5-6-1767; Samuel, b 7-8-1735; Jonathan, b 8-9-1737; Joshua, b 12-28-1740; Martha, b 1-21-1743; Nathan, b 7-16-1744; Aaron, b 10-14-1746; Rebeckah, b 7-27-1749; Elizabeth, b 6-26-1756.†

Joseph, Sr., Alloways Creek Precinct, will 8th of 5th mo. (July), 1742, affirmed 3-28-1745. Chd. Broadway, Joseph, Peter, and Sarah Ware.‡

Peter, Alloways Creek, int. 11-15-1749. Sarah Stretch, adm.‡

String, Peter, Morice River, int. 11-15-1748. Margaret String, adm.‡

Stromp, Christopher, m Mary Long, 1-11-1748.*

Stubings, Henry, Allowayes Creek, will 16th of 6th mo. (Aug.), 1688, rec. 5-20-1689. Chd. Samuel and Henry (both under age); bro. John Stubings of Bumstead, Cambridgeshire, Eng.§

Stubbines, Henry, m Rebeckah Daniels, both of Elsenborough 4-1-1737.†

Henry, m Mary Vickery, both of Elsenboro, 9-24-1742.†

Stubbins, Samuel, Elsenburg, will 2-25-1713/14. Wf. Sarah; son Henry.**

Samuel. Wf. Sarah; chd. Elizabeth, b 12-20-1710; Henry, b 6-4-1712, d 6-7-1761.†

Sullivan, Daniel, Alloways Creek, int. 6-27-1748.‡

Dennis, Alloways Creek, int. 5-22-1749.‡

Summerill, William, emig. from Ireland abt. 1725, locating in Penns Neck. Wf. Mary.††

Surridge, John, mariner, Salem Town, will 12th of 10th mo. (Dec.), 1729, affirmed 11-4-1734. Wf. Elizabeth; cousin Jonathan Suradge.‡

Swane (Swine, Sweney, Swinny), **Owen,** Penns Neck, will 1-9-1728/9, pr. 1-28-1728/9. Wf. Elizabeth, wid. of Thomas Pedrick; son Mils; son-in-law (?stepson) Thomas Pedrick ‡

Syears, Joseph, Cohansey. Bond of Margerett Syears, adm., 1-24-1715/16.**

Tankersly, Elizabeth, wid., Salem, will 10-28-1711, pr. 11-29-1711. Dau. Mary Sherron; grandson Roger Sherron.**

Tappen, Jacob, husb. Cohansey, will 11-8-1732, affirmed 2-5-

1732. Wf. Mary; dau.-in-law Mercy Williams; grandson Joseph Hodge.‡

Tarbel, Nathan, m Elizabeth Robinson, 10-3-1745. Chd. Abraham, bap. 11-15-1747; Keturah, bap. 9-17-1749*

Tate, William, m Frances Daily, 8-11-1733.¶

Taylor, John, Cohansey, will 7-11-1719, pr. 8-29-1729. Wf. Martha.‡

Test, Francis, m Elizabeth Bacon. 12-3-1724. Chd. Thomas, b 9-22-1725; Rachel, b 8-2-1727; Benjamin, b 8-14-1734; Elizabeth, b 12-18-1731; John, b 4-18-1734; Ruth, b 2-10-1741; Leatitia, b 11-20-1742; Francis, b 2-4-1744; Abner, b 8-23-1747.†

Tewksbury, Thomas, husb., inv. 10-25-1700. Wf. Ann.§

Thompson, Andrew, s of Thomas, b at Kirkfenton, Yorkshire, Eng., in 1637. On 9-29-1658, with wf. Elizabeth and sons John and Andrew, re. to Ireland. On 7-11-1664, Andrew m Isabelle, dau. of Humphrey Marshall, b in Silby, near Lestershire. Chd. Elizabeth, b in Parish Donard, Co. Wicklow, Ire, 8-15-1666; William, b do., 8-9-1669; Andrew, b do, 11-13-1676. Andrew re. with wf. and sd. chd. to West Jersey, sailing in the "Mary of Dublin," and landed at Elsinburgh, 12-23-1677. John, s of Andrew and Isabelle Thompson, was b at Elsinborough, 4-23-1684.†

Andrew, Elsenburgh, husb., will 29th of 10th mo., 1694, rec. 11-9-1696. Chd. William, Andrew, Elizabeth, wf. of Isaac Smart; and John; bro. John Thompson.§

Andrew. Wf. Grace; chd. Thomas, b 11-28-1707; Sarah, b 2-8-1709; Abraham, b 12-26-1710; Joshua, b 2-2-1713; Thomas, b 7-21-1715; Rebeckah, b 11-3-1717/18; Abraham, b 5-27-1721.†

Andrew. Wf Rebeckah; chd. Jonathan, b 9-16-1697; Hannah, b 1-12-1698/9; Isabel, b 10-22-1700; Andrew, b 2-2-1704.†

Andrew, Jr., Elsenburrow, will 4th of 5th mo. (Sept.), 1727. Wf. Grace; chd. Andrew, Joshua, Hannah Cook, Thomas, Sarah and Abraham; bro. John Thompson.‡

Andrew. Wf. Ann; chd. Joshua, b 1-17-1729.†

Benjamin, b 11th of 8th mo., 1719, s of William and Hannah Thompson, m Elizabeth, dau. of Joseph Ware, 2d, in 1745. Chd. Benjamin, m —— Willis.‖

Benjamin. Wf. Elizabeth; chd. Millicent, b 6-12-1747, d 6-23-1776; Benjamin, b Dec. 1756; Hannah, b 11-14-1749/50; Sarah, b 3-26-1759.†

Francis. m Ann Craig, 2-2-1748. Chd. Mary, bap. 5-4-1749.*

Isaac, weaver, Alloways Creek, int. 9-20-1740.‡

James. Wf. Ann; chd. Jane, b 9-28-1702; Ann, b 1-5-1704; John, b 8-18-1707; Elizabeth, 12-3-1709; James, b 8-26-1712.†

James, Jr., s of James and Ann Thompson, m Sarah Wood (others say Wossley), and re. to Delaware.‖

James, Elsenborrough Precinct, inv. 1st of 3d mo., 1712.**

James. Wf. Eupho; chd. William and Elizabeth, twins, bap. 8-17-1746; Samuel and James, both bap. 11-11-1744.*

John, s Thomas, b at Kirkfenton, Yorkshire, Eng., in May, 1635. In 1658, with wf. Elizabeth and sons John and Andrew, he re. to Ireland. In 1665, John m Jane, dau. of Thomas Humbles, late of Co. Durham, Eng., but now dwelling in Ireland. Chd. Thomas, b in Parish of Donard, Co. Wicklow, Ireland, 1666; James, b 1668; Ann, b 1672; Mary, b 10-15-1675. John Thompson came to West Jersey with wf. and said chd., in the "Mary of Dublin," landing at Elsenburg, 12-22-1677 †

John, Elsenburrow, yeo., will 24th of 6th mo. (Aug.), 1715, pr. 1-27-1715/16. Wf. Sarah; chd. James, who has s John and James and daus not named; Thomas, who has dau. Sarah and others not named; and Mary, wf. of Richard Woodnut.**

Joshua, m Sarah Hill, 4-13-1733.¶

Joshua, s of Andrew and Grace Thompson, b 2-2-1713, m 1st Sarah ———; 2d Elizabeth Gibson. Chd. by Sarah—Andrew, b 29th of 5th mo., 1739; Sarah, b 24th of 12th mo., 1742. Chd. by Elizabeth—Joshua and Rebecca, twins, b 8th of 6th mo., 1748; John, b 7th of 4th mo., 1752; Joseph, b 23th of 3d mo., 1756.‖

Joshua. Wf. Elizabeth; chd. Rebeckah, b 6-10-1745; Joseph, b 6-8-1748; John, b 4-17-1752, d 12-28-1824; Joseph, b 3-26-1736, d 3-23-1778.†

Joseph, of Alloways Creek, m Mary Condon, of Mannington, 5-9-1747. Chd. Rachel, b 1-26-1748; Samuel, b 12-18-1749/50; Hannah, b 1-26-1752; William, b 3-20-1754; Prudence, b 4-24-1756; Mary, b 8-12-1758; Rebeckah, b 11-2-1760; Elizabeth, b 1-4-1762 †

Joseph. Wf. Sarah; chd. Elizabeth, b 8-1-1716; Jane, b 1-4-1718/19; William, b 8-30-1920; Martha, b 11-31-1724; Sarah, b 5-31-1726; Grace, b 2-15-1730; Susanna, b 6-15-1734 †

Joseph, Alloways Creek, will 12-17-1739, pr. 4-25-1740. Wf. Sarah; chd. William, Joseph, Elizabeth, Jane, Martha, Sarah, Grace, Mary and Susannah ‡

Lydia, Elsinburgh, inv. 4-20-1726.‡

Samuel, s of William and Hannah, b in 1707, m Edith, dau. of William Tyler, 2d. Chd. Samuel, a tanner, and Rebecca, wf. of David Allen, of Mannington ‖

Samuel. Wf. Edith; chd. Thomas, b 6-17-1732; Hannah, b 1-10-

1734; Mary, b 11-10-1735; Anne, b 10-14-1737; James, b 11-21-1739/40; Samuel and Edith, twins, b 1-16-1742; Rebeckah, b 11th mo., 1748, m David Allen.†

Samuel, Alloways Creek, will 12-17-1749, affirmed 2-14-1749/50. Wf. Edith; chd. Thomas, Samuel (both under age), Ann, Mary and Rebekah.‡

Samuel, int. 7-19-1733   Abigail Thompson, adm.‡

Sarah, wid., Elsenburgh, will 5-23-1720, pr. 10-25-1721. Chd. Thomas, who has daus. Lydia, and Rachel Taylor; and James, who has chd. John, Jane, Ann, Elizabeth and James; son-in-law Samuel Stubins, who has s Henry; bro. James Leonard.‡

Thomas. Wf. Rebeccah; chd. Sarah, b 7-27-1692; Rebeccah, b 12-24-1694/5.†

Thomas. Wf. Dorithy; chd. Rachel, b 1-14-1696/7; John, b 4-7-1698; Lydia, b 4-13-1702; Mary, b 9-10-1703.†

Thomas. Wf. Jane; dau. Sarah, b 5-17-1697.†

Thomas, Anns Grove, will 12th of 1st mo., 1713/14, pr. 5-31-1714. Wf. Sarah; chd. Sarah, Rachel, Ledieth, Mary (last 3 under age); father John Thompson; cousin Andrew Thompson.‡

Thomas. Wf. Mary; chd. Joshua, b 12-9-1739/40; John, b 4-28-1741; Joshua, b 7-30-1743; Thomas, b 10-19-1745; Sarah, b 9-5-1747; Mary, b 9-2-1749; Grace, b 5-22-1751.†

Thomas, joiner, Salem, will 12-24-1747. Wf. Mary; chd. Daniel, Joshua, Mary; bro. Joshua Thompson.§

William, s of Andrew and Isabella. 1st wf. Sarah; chd. Joseph. 2d wf. Jane; chd. William. 3d wf Hannah; chd. Jane, Susanna, Samuel, Mary, Rebecca and Benjamin.‖

William. Wf. Sarah; chd. Joseph, b 1-22-1792/3.†

William. Wf. Jane; chd. William, b 3-16-1695.†

William. Wf. Hannah; chd. Jane, b 7-29-1700; Susannah, b 8-26-1704; Samuel, b 9-6-1707; Mary, b 11-2-1710; Rebeckah, b 12-19-1714; Benjamin, b 3-11-1719.†

William. Wf. Elizabeth; chd. Rebeckah, b 8-25-1720; Nathaniel, b 10-9-1722; Isaac, b 12-20 1724; James, b 11-24-1726; Andrew, b 3-4-1729; Hannah, b 2-3-1735; Elizabeth, b 7-9-1737.†

William, Alloways Creek, will 5-15-1733, affirmed 4-25-1734. Chd. Joseph, William, Samuel, Benjamin, Sarah and Rebeckah; grandson Samuel Test.‡

Thornton, Francis, will 8th of 10th mo. (Dec.), 1687, rec. 2-23-1687/8. Sister Mary Clemont.§

Tindall, Benjamin. Wf. Hester; chd. Joseph, b 6-16-1749; Mary, b 10-7-1751.†

Richard, Tindall's Bowery, Mannenton Precinct, will 1!-10-1697, pr. 5-28-1698. Wf. Elizabeth.§

Toersen (Tewlson), **Wooley**, husb., Penns Neck, will 11-11-1694, rec. 4-12-1695, Wf. Sarah; chd. Fabus, Saffredus and Sarah §

Tome (alias Tossy), **Joseph**, m Hannah Brown, 7-12-1742. Chd. Mary, bap. 1-1-1743/4; Elizabeth, bap. 4-14-1745; Joseph, bap. 7-24-1746; Hannah, bap. 6-5-1748.

Tossy, Joseph. Wf. Hannah; dau, Sarah, bap. 8-26-1750.*

Townsend, Jacob, blacksmith, int. 5-31-1740. Wf. Mary,‡
James, inv. 12-5-1705. Wf. Rebecca.§

Trafford, Samuel, Salem, will 5-20-1714, p;. 6-12-1714. Chd. Thomas, Elizabeth Willson, Joseph, Sarah, Rachel, Samuel, Rebecka, Esther.‡

Trenchard, George, Sr., yeo., Salem Town, will 4-18-1712, pr. 5-1-1712. Chd. George, Edward, John and Jone.**
George, Jr., will pr. 12-9-1728. Wf. Mary; s John; bro. Edward Trenchard; cousins Mary and John Thompson.**

Tully, Francis. Wf. Hannah; chd. Phebe, bap. 8-10-1740; Azubah, bap. 5-2-1742; Samuel, bap. 11-11-1744; Mary, bap. 8-2-1747; Ann, bap. 5-28-1749.*
Robert, m Phebe Conkelyn, 3-23-1748. Son Gideon, bap. 3-19-1748/9.*

Turner, John, innkeeper, int. 1-23-1740. Sarah Turner, adm.‡
Hannah, int. 2-14-1734.‡

Tussey, Catharine, int. 2-23-1749.‡

Tyler, Benjamin, m Naomi Denn, both of Alloways Creek, 7-3-1746. Chd. Elizabeth, b 2-28-1748; Rachel, b 7-12-1751; John, b 2-1-1753; Leatitia, b 11-9-1755.†
Enoch, int. 4-2-1746.‡
James, Alloways Creek, s of William, 2d, and Mary Tyler, b 30th of 12th mo., 1720, m Martha Simpson. Chd. James, and Ruth wf. of John Ware.||
John, Alloways Creek, int. 9-5-1732. Wf Rachel.§
Philip, s of William Tyler 1st, b 1692 near Salem, m 1st, Elizabeth, dau. of John Maddox Denn. Chd. Enoch, and Elizabeth, wf of —— Watson. He m 2d, —— Moore. Chd. Rachel, and a dau. not named, who m Ephraim Sayre.||
Philip, will 8-1-1737, affirmed 1-10-1737. Chd. Philip and Enoch.‡
Samuel, s of William, 2d, and Mary Tyler, b 26th of 10th mo. 1723,

m, in 1751, Ann, dau. of John Mason, Jr. Chd. William, John, Mary, Samuel and Rebecca.‖

William. Wf. Joanna; chd. Mary. b in Old England, 11th mo., 1677; William, b 7-5-1680; John, b 5-2-1682; Johanna, b 2-2-1684.†

William. Wf. Elizabeth; chd. Katherine, b in Salem County 6-13-1690; Philip, b 3-17-1692; Elizabeth, b 7-24-1695; Rebeckah, b 2-19-1698.†

William, s of William and Joanna Tyler, d in 1733; m Mary Abbott. Chd. William, b 2d of 5th mo., 1712; Edith, b 24th of 11th mo. 1714, m Samuel Thompson; Rebecca, b 29th of 3d mo., 1716; Mary, b 16th of 1st mo., 1718; James, b 30th of 12th mo., 1720; Samuel, b 26th of 10th mo., 1723. His wf. m Robert Townsend of Cape May, in 1735.‖

William, yeo., Alloways Creek, will 2-28-1700/1, rec. 6-20-1701. Chd. Philipp, John, William, Mary, wf. of Abel Nicholson; Joan, Katherine, Elizabeth and Rebecka.§

William, 3d, s of William, Jr., and Mary (Abbott) Tyler, m Elizabeth, dau. of Joseph and Sarah Thompson, b 1st of 8th mo., 1716. Chd. Sarah, m Samuel, s of Joseph and Mary Stewart; Rebecca, m William Abbott.‖

William, Alloways Creek, will 11-29-1732, affirmed 3-8-1733/4. Chd. William, Editha, wf. of Sammel Thompson; Rebecca, James and Samuel; wf. Mary.‡

William, m Elizabeth Thompson, June, 1737.¶

William, Alloways Creek, will 6-10-1749, affirmed 7-17-1749. Chd. Editha (youngest dau.), Mary, Grace, Rebecca and Sarah; bro.-in-law Samuel Thompson.‡

Unson, Erick, planter, Finns Point, will spoken 1-1-1684/5. Five chd not named.§

Mathias, Castiana Neck on Fenwick's River or Salem Creek, planter, will 2-14-1684/5. Chd. Woola Matheson, Michael the 3d son, Eric the 4th son, and 6 not named.§

Vance, John, mill whrite, adm granted 11-2-1703. Wf. Prudence.§

Vanculin, Jacobus, will 7-22-1745, pr. 4-16-1747. Son William; grandson Andrew Matson, his dau's. son.‡

William, Penns Neck, will 12-17-1746, pr. 2-19-1746. Chd. John, Jacob, William, Andrew, Catherine, Rebecca, Sarah and Rachel; father Jacobus Vanculin.‡

Van de Vear, Catteren, Penns Neck, inv. 1-23-1727/8.**
Jacob, Jr., Penns Neck, inv. 5-5-1729. Wf. Margreatt.**
Margreat, Penns Neck, inv. 10-17-1729.‡

Van de Veer, Jacobes, farmer, Penns Neck, will 8-15-1726, pr.

12-7-1726. Wf. Cattrain; chd. Jacob, William, Henry, (?stepsons) Thomas and Andrew Tosaway.‡

Vandevere, Henry, Penns Neck, will 2-22-1748/9, pr. 3-12-1848/9. Wf. Sarah; s Jacob.‡

Vandick, Stephen, int. 2-11-1748. Wf. Irane.‡

Vaneman, John, Penns Neck, husb., int. 5-9-1746.‡
William, Pilesgrove Precinct, will 11-1-1748, pr. 11-30-1748. Wf. Magdalen; chd. Jacob, William. Andrew, Elizabeth Lorence, and Rebecca.‡

Vanemen, John, Penns Neck, yeo, will 3-30-1719, pr. 11-10-1719. Wf. Cattren; chd. Johannes, others not named; wf.'s bro. Martin Johnson.**

Venemy (Vaneman), **Johannes,** inv. sworn to 9-17-1706.**

Vanhist, Rainier, int. 4-6-1747.‡

Van Hyst, Rennere, yeo., will 2-1-1697/8, rec. 8-22-1698. Wf. Elizabeth; chd. Rennere, Barbara, Elizabeth and Gertrude (all under age).§

Vanmeter, Henry, m Sarah Elwell, 9-4-1727.¶
Henry, Jr. Wf. Rebekah; chd. Isaac, bap. 9-26-1742.*
Henry. Wf. Mary; chd. Fetters, bap. 4-12-1741; Mary, bap. 1-16-1742/3; Benjamin, bap. 11-11-1744; Jacob, bap. 4-10-1748.*
Joseph, m Hannah Vial, 4-28-1745. Chd. Elizabeth, Henry and Sarah, all bap. 7-16-1749.*

Vanniman, Johannes, yeo., will pr. 5-7-1707. Wf. Elizabeth; chd. John, Wolow, Henry, Peter, Garrat, and 2 not named.‡

Viccary, James, planter, inv. 4-16-1692. Wf. Judith.§

Vickary, Edward. Wf. Sarah; chd. Hannah, b 10-21-1723; Rebeckah, b 12-13-1725.†
Richard, will pr. 9-30-1714. Wf. Elizabeth; chd. Rachel and Sarah; bro. Edward Vickery.‡

Vickery, John, single man, Penns Neck, int. 3-23-1735/6.‡
Samuel, Penns Neck, husb., will 6-4-1726, pr. 5-1-1727. Wf. Elizabeth; chd. Edward, Thomas (both under age) and others not named.‡
Thomas, bricklayer, Penns Neck, will 8-9-1725, pr. 9-23-1725. Wf. Margaret; chd. John, William, Jane and Margaret (all under age); nephew William Vickery, who has son Thomas; bro. Edward Vickery.‡
William, husb., Penns Neck, will 9-18-1738, pr. 1738. Sisters Jane and Margaret; father Thomas Vickery; father-in-law William Mecum.‡

Vickey (Vickery), **Edward**, inv. 5-3-1749.§

James, husb., Mannington, will 1-6-1731/2, affirmed 2-15-1731/2. Chd. Elizabeth, James (under age), and Edward; bro. Edward Vickey.‡

Waddington, Jonathan, Alloways Creek Twp., farmer, will 15th of 9th mo. (November, 1748, affirmed 2-15-1748. Chd. William, Hannah, Jane, Mary and Ellzabeth.‡

Jonathan, s of William. Chd. Hannah, m Maurice Beesley; Ann, m 1750, John Baracliff; Elizabeth, m Edward, s of Jonathan Bradway; Jane, m Bradway Keasbey, Jonathan.‖

William, French Huguenot, emig. 1680. Son Jonathan.‖

Wade, Edward, of Buttolph, Oldgate, London; wf. Prudence; on "Griffin", with servants, Nathaniel Champney, Jr., Joseph Ware, John Burton and Francis Smithey; ar. Salem, 9-23-1675.†

Edward, Munmouth River, yeo., will 12th of 9th mo. (Nov.) 1692, rec. 12-4-1694. Wf. Prudence, bro. Samuel Wade, who has s Samuel.§

Joseph, cordwainer, Salem Town, int. 3-12-1731. Wf. Hannah, m Renier Gregory.‡

Prudence, Alloways Creek, wid., will 2d of 2d mo. (Apr.), 1698, rec. 5-27-1698. Bro.-in-law Samuel Wade.§

Robert, Edward and Samuel Wade came in the "Griffith" in 1675. Robert went to Upland, now Chester; Edward located at Salem, and Samuel settled on Alloways Creek.††

Samuel, s of John, b in Northampton, Eng., 1645; ar. on "Griffin," 8-23-1675; wf. Jane, dau. of Thomas Smith, b at West Chester, 1645, and came in the "Henry & Anne." Son Samuel, b 6-1-1685.†

Samuel, Alloways Creek, will 17th of 5th mo. (July), 1698. Wf. Jeane; s Samuel.§

Samuel, s of Samuel and Jane Wade. Chd. Joseph, Samuel, dau. not named, m James Barker; Esther, m Samuel Lewis; Mary, m John Stewart.‖

Samuel. Wf. Mary; chd. Joseph, b 7-28-1703.†

Samuel, Alloways Creek, will 18th of 5th mo. (July), 1734, affirmed 7-29-1734. Chd. Lydia Tomlinson, Mary, Esther, Hannah and Mellscent; son-in-law Joseph Tomlinson.‡

Waid, Joseph. Wf Hannah; dau Milisent, b 3-21-1729.†

Wakefield, Elizabeth, Elsenburrough, wid., will 8-18-1727, pr. 9-13-1727. Daus. Rachel, Mary, Elizabeth, Prissilla and Mary Anne; granddaus. Elisabeth Symms and Jane ———; son-in-law John Symms.‡

Walcott, Samuel, Penns Neck, tailor, will 12-16-1728, pr. 12-28-1728. Dau. Mary.*

Walden, William. Wf. Hannah; dau. Elizabeth, b 3-21-1707.†

William, Middle Neck, will 2-24-1720/1, pr. 4-5-1721. Wf. Mary; chd. William, John, Mary and Rebeckah (last 3 under age); son-in-law (?stepson) John Winton (under age).**

Walker, Daniel, Fairfield Twp., int. 5-1-1750.‡

John, Elsingborrow Precinct, will 2-26-1704/5. Wf. Elizabeth; chd. John (under age) and Elizabeth.‡

Joseph, Manington, weaver, will 3-25-1733, pr. 4-25-1733 Wf. Mary; chd. Ann, Hannah, William and Sarah (all under age).‡

Wallace, Henry, int. 3-5-1743. Elizabeth Wallace, adm.‡

Walling, John, Cohansey, will 6-1-1743, pr. 4-25-1745. Chd. John, Jonathan and Hannah; bro. Thomas Walling; sister Mary Bowring.‡

Jonathan, Bethel, will 7-18-1719, pr. 4-4-1721. Wf. Elizabeth; chd. John, Thomas, Elias, Mary, wf. of Dan Bowin; Rebecah, wf. of Charles Dennes; and Phebe.‡

Thomas, carpenter, will 5-19-1724, pr. 10-22-1724. Wf. Sarah; chd. Thomas, Elisha, John, James, Joseph, Benjamin, Rebaca, Abigal, wf. of John Bedient; and William.**

Thomas, int. 1-21-1733. Wf. Bathinpleoth.‡

Thomas, Cohansey, will 10-6-1747, pr. 6-7-1748. Wf. Sarah: chd. Anna, Mary, Jonathan and Thomas.‡

Thomas, int. 3-8-1750.§

Walty, Andreas, m Margaret Hoffham, 3-10-1745/6.¶

Wamsley, Henry. Wf. Dynah; chd. Nathaniel, b 11-10-1700; George, b 7-1-1702; Jonathan, b 10-16-1704; Ann, b 9-25-1707.†

Ware, Jacob. Wf. Naomi; s Richard, b 3-2-1744.†

Jacob, Jr., Greenwich Twp., int. 5-19-1749. Wf. Phebe.‡

James, came as servant of Edward Wade, in 1675.††

John, Cohansey, will 5-1-1734, pr. 6-20-1734. Wf. Bathsheba; chd. John, Hannah, Roda, Elnathan (under age), Mary and Abigail ‡

John, m Elizabeth Fogg, 5-13-1749.†

Joseph. Wf. Martha; dau. Sarah, b 7-5-1686.†

Joseph, in 1683, m Martha Goff. Chd. Joseph, b 1684; Sarah, b 1686; John, b circa 1688.‖

Joseph. Wf. Mary; dau. Prudence, b 11-12-1707.†

Joseph, Sr., Alloways Creek, will 3-28-1711, d Mar. 30th. Wf. Mary; chd. Joseph and Patience (under age); sons-in-law (?stepsons) William and Nathaniel Williams.**

Joseph. Wf. Elizabeth; chd. Mary, b 12-22-1735/6; Sarah, b 8/22-

1737; Hannah, b 7-4-1739; Rebeckah, b 11-9-1741/2; Joseph, b 3-26-1744; Elijah, b 1-30-1748 O. S , d 12-2-1807.†

Josiah, Cohansey, tailor, will 4-23-1749   Bro. Thomas; sisters Phebe, Amey and Elizabeth.***

Solomon. Wf. Sarah; chd. Elizabeth, b 9-30 1743; Peter, b 8-25-1741; Job, b 8-10-1745, d 2-19-1765; Hannah, b.7-25-1747, d 11-7-1765; Elisha, b 4-22-1749, d 2-1-1769; Bathsheba, b 3-5-1753; Sarah, b 6-12-1753; Solomon, b 7-17-1760.†

Warrick, Thomas. Wf. Hannah; dau. Mary, b 11-12-1705.†

Warner, Simon, Alloways Creek, will 7-12-1731, pr. 6-7-1735. Wf. Susannah; chd. William, Simon, George (all under age), Hannah and Sarah.§

William, Monmouth River, cordwainer, non. will rec. 7-4-1691. Son Simon; son-in-law (?stepson) John Nicholas §

Watson, Abraham, shoemaker, int. 11-4-1749. Margaret Watson, adm.‡

Thomas, Greenwitch, will 11-16-1694, rec. 4-12-1695. Wf. Sarah; chd. William, Thomas and Sarah.§

Thomas, cordwainer, adm. granted 11-17-1729.‡

William, Greenwich, will 3-9-1742, affirmed 4-30-1743. Wf. Sarah; chd. William, Isaac, Rachel Shepherd, Lurane Coffen, Sarah Martin, Hannah Wheaton, Mary and Elizabeth.‡

Weaks, Amos, m Deborah Nealson, 12-31-1742.*

Weatheriell, John, Mannington, tanner, bond of adm.11-19-1728. Wf. Anne.**

Weatherill, Thomas, m Sarah Hale, 1-19-1748.¶

Webb, Edward, Mannenton Creek, will 3-26-1688, rec. 9-26-1688. Wf. Jane; bro. Samuel Webb of Berkshire, Eng.§

Elias, Mannenton Creek, non. will 1-10-1694/5; inv. 3-11-1694/5. Wf. Jane.§

William, Mannington Precinct, glover, will 9-15-1721, pr. 11-11-1721. Chd. William and Thomas.‡

Welch, Thomas, Penns Neck, weaver, int. 2-29-1747/8.‡

Wescote, David. Wf. Rachel; chd David, bap. 6-21-1741; John, bap. 4-22-1744; Abinadab, bap. 6-8-1746.*

Westcot, Ebenezer, Fairfield Precinct, husb, will 1-7-1748/9; pr. 2-25-1748/9. Wf. Barbary; chd. Ebenezer, Foster, Samuel, Jonathan, David, Joseph, Abigail, Rhode, Mary, Phebe and Joanna.‡

Westcott (Waistcoate), **Daniel,** Caesaria River, will 11-30-1702, pr. 2-14-1703/4. Wf. Abigail; chd. Samuel, Daniel, Ebenezer, Mary, Joanna Foster and Abigail Lummus; cousin James Weed of Stamford, New England.‡

Daniel, Cohansey, will 10-14-1742, pr. 12-3-1742. Wf. Elizabeth; chd. Daniel, Henry, and Rachel Percel.‡

Weslake, Samuel, Pilesgrove, inv. 5-5-1726. Ann Weslake, adm.**

Westland, Oliver, joiner, Penns Neck, int. 4-17-1734.§

Wetherbey, John, m Mary Colyer, 3-19-1749.¶

Wetherby, Daniel, m Mary Cox, 9-30-1745.*
Robert, int. 1-15-1735.‡

Wethman, William, Cohansie, will 12-1-1712, pr. 11-16-1714. Wf. Elizabeth; chd. William, John, Elizabeth and Thomas.‡

Wettenberey (Wittenberry), **Jacob,** Penns Neck, flatman, int. 11-7-1748.‡

Wheaten, Jonathan, Cohansie, inv. 10-23-1713.**
Noah, Cohansey, blacksmith, will 12-20-1715, pr. 5-5-1716 Wf. Sarah; chd. Isaac, Noah and Sarah; bro. Samuel Bowin.**

Wheller (Whealer, Wheeler), **John,** Cohansey, int. 11-17 1730. Wf. Rebecca.‡

Whitacar, Nathaniel, s of Richard, Jr., m 1st Mary Ann Dixon, 18th of 11th mo., 1729. Chd. Ambrose, Lemuel and Lewis W. He m 2d Ruth Buck. Chd. Sarah, Hannah, wf. of Ephraim Foster; Daniel, and Ruth, wf. of Josiah Harris.‖

Whital, John, will 12-15-1733, affirmed 2-14-1733. Wf. Elizabeth; chd. William and John (both under age) ‡

White, Christopher, s of Thomas, b at Comren, Co. Cumberland, Eng., abt. 1642, re. to London, 1666; abt. 1668 m Ester Beetle (Hester Biddle—*London Friends' Records*), b in Stepney Parish, near London, dau. of John Wieat. In 2d mo., 1677, came with s John, b at Poplar, in Stepney, 9-18-1663; Esther, b at Shadwell, near London, abt. 1669; Josiah, b in Brooke Street, Rathlief, near London, abt. 1675; Christopher, b at Salem, 2-5-1678.†

Christopher, Alloways Creek, will 13th of 7th mo. (Sept.), 1693, rec 12-28-1793. Wf. Easter; chd. Easter, Josiah, Joseph (last 2 under age); grandson George Beetle.§

Hester, Munmouth River, wid., will 11th of 3d mo. (May), 1698, rec. 6-24-1698 Dau. Hester Harrison, who has chd Joseph and Sarah Harrison; sons Josiah White and John Biddle.§

John, m Mary Hall, 3-4-1728.¶

John. Wf. Elizabeth; dau. Hannah, b 1-9-1738/9.†

John joiner; int. 3-25-1740. Wf. Elizabeth.‡

Joseph, s of Samuel and Reines White, b 1-20-1651/2, at Sulgrave, North Hampshire, Eng., re to Ireland, 7-25-1672, and afterwards m Elizabeth, dau of Arthur and Elizabeth Church, who came from Dolbay of the Woulds, in Lestershire, Eng., to Ireland. Joseph and his wf. came from Carthalow, Ire., took ship at Dublin for West Jersey, and ar. at Elsinburgh, 9-17-1681, with servants Hugh Middleton, Matthias Belles and Hannah Ashbury. Joseph and Elizabeth had dau. Reines, b 9-17-1681, being the day they ar. in Elsinburgh.†

Joseph. Wf. Elizabeth; son Joseph, b 11-29-1692.†

Joseph, Jr. Wf. Mary; chd. Joseph, b 10-21-1718; John, b 3-19-1717.†

Josiah, Alloways Creek, will 2-19-1713/14, pr. 5-10-1714, Wf. Hannah.‡

Josiah, Alloways Creek, will 2-19-1713/14, pr. 5-10-1714. Wf. Hannah.‡

Josiah. Wf. Hannah; chd. Christopher, b 6-23-1699; Josiah, b 6-21-1705; Hester, b 10-6-1707; Hannah, b 2-22-1710; Abigail, b 6-11-1613.†

Whittall, Elizabeth, wid., will 16th of 9th mo. (Nov.), 1733, pr. 12-31-1740. Chd. William, John (both under age) Esther, Elizabeth and Rhoda.‡

Elizabeth, spinster, int. 3-2-1740. Bro.-in-law James Breeden of Alloways Creek ‡

Whittan, James. Wf. Sarah; chd. Ann, b 12th or 15th of 10th mo., 1707; Joseph, b 9-9-1709.†

Whitton, Catherine, Salem, wid., will 7th of 1st mo. (Mar.), 1732, affirmed 5-19-1733. Bro. Edward Williams; sister Elizabeth Loyd; mother-in-law Jane Williams; cousins Rebecka Key, Elizabeth Simmons, Samuel Cripps, Richard Darkin (under age), Hannah Darkin, and Gwen Evans.‡

Christopher, inv. 9-19-1687.§

James, will 11-3-1732, affirmed 1-10-1732. Wf. Catherine; s Joseph.‡

Joseph, will 3-2-1732, pr. 3-12 1732. Mother Catherine Whitton; uncles David Morris, and John Darkin, who has chd. Jael, Richard and Joseph.‡

Wiat, Bartholomew. Wf. Elizabeth; s Bartholomew b 5-20 1731.†

Wiggins, David, Penns Neck, will 11-28-1744, pr. 12-6-1744. Rebecca Wiggins, adm.§

James, cordwainer, will 3-14-1727/8, pr. 3-29-1728. Wf. Elizabeth; chd. Hannah, James and Mary.‡

Wild, John, int. 5-12-1736.‡

Wilkinson, James, laborer, Salem, bond of adm. 4-28-1722.**
William, m Mary Nickson, 6-8-1689.¶

Willcox, Mary, dau. of Robert, of Whitechapel, maidservant, came on the "Dorothy," ar. Philadelphia, 8-14-1685.†

Wilder, John, Penns Neck, int. 10-21-1742. Wf. Margaret.‡

Williams, John, the "predecessor of Henry Syckes, of Alloways Creek," will 3-3-1713/14, pr. 3-22-1714. Wf. Mary; dau. Sarah; son-in-law (?stepson) James Sykes; wife's sister Rebecka Etteridge.‡
John, Alloways Creek, will 8-7-1718, pr. 1-15- 1721/2.‡
John, Seeder Run (Alloways Creek), will 3-30-1727, pr. 5-31-1731. Wf. Katherine.‡
Thomas, Mannenton Creek, inv. 1-18-1696/7.§

Willis, William, Alloways Creek, will 11-21-1694, rec. 1-8-1694/5. Wf. Elizabeth; s William.§
William, Sr., Alloways Creek, carpenter, will 6-21-1740, affirmed 8-14-1740. Wf. Mary; chd. William, Stephen (under age), Elizabeth, Esther, Rachel and Lydia.‡

Willson, Thomas, comer of wool, bond of adm. 2-18-1728/9.**

Wilson, Enoch, m Lydia ———, 1-4-1741/2.*

Windrwa (Windrew, Windrw, Wamdrw, Vandrew), **Andrew,** minister of the Gospel, inv. 2-20-1728/9; wf. Elizabeth.**

Windsor, Solomon, ward, 1-19-1733.‡

Winter, Joshua, Cohansey, int. 12-26-1734.‡

Winton, Joseph, int. 4-28-1735.‡
Nicholas, m Dorothy Davis, 1-16-1699/1700.¶

Wistar, Caspar, buttonmaker, native of Germany, emig. to Pennsylvania in 1717. Chd. Richard, Caspar and Srrah.‖
Richard, s of Caspar who was b in Heidelberg, Germany, and emig. to Pennsylvania, and Katharine Johnson of Germantown, b in 1727, m Sarah, dau. of Bartholomew Wyatt of Mannington Twp., in 1751. Chd. Caspar, Bartholomew, Richard, John, Caspar (a second son), Thomas, Elizabeth and Catharine.††

Witacar, Richard, Cohansey, cordwainer, will 6-5-1718. Wf. Abigail; chd. Richard, Thomas, Katterine and Nathaniel. (12-26-1721, bond of Hanah Whitacar, wid., adm. of estate of Richard W., her late husband.)‡

Wood, Gabriel, Mannington, husb., will 1-12-1732, pr. 1-29-1732. Chd. Gabriel, Elizabeth, Joseph, and Hannah (under age); bro. Joseph Wood.‡

James, m Margaret Booth, both of Cohansey, 8-16-1744.*

Jeremiah. Son Jeremiah, bap. 11-30-1740.*

Jonathan, Stow Creek, inv. 8-22-1715.**

Jonathan, Cohansey, carpenter, will 8-2-1727, pr. 9-7-1727. Wf. Mary; chd Samuel, Obadiah, Jonathan, John and David (all under age).‡

Joseph, Mannington, int. 8-10-1743. Wf. Katherine.‡

Richard. Wf. Priscilla; chd. Jane, b 4-18-1723; Richard, b 1-18-1728; Leatitia, b 2-5-1730; Ruth, b 1-16-1732; Priscilia, b 1 4-1734.†

Woodhouse, Anthony, Cohansey, will 28th of 9th mo. (Nov.); 1694, rec. 1-8-1694 5. Chd. Samuel, John and Thomas (last 2 under age); son-in-law William Remmington.§

Hannah, spinster, Cohansey, bond of adm. 11-28-1726.‡

Samuel, m Ann Hudson, 1-22-1694 5.¶

Samuel, Cohansey, will 1-10-1718, pr. 9-23-1718. Wf. Ann; chd. Anthony, Samuel, John, Job and Hannah (last 4 under age).‡

Woodnut, Grace, wid. of Richard, inv. 10th of 1st mo. (March), 1690 1.§

Joseph. Wf. Rachel; chd. Thomas, b 3-12-1724; Mary, b 4-19-1727; Hannah, b 9-11-1729; Richard, b 1-10-1731.2; Joseph, b 11-8-1734,5.†

Joseph, s of Richard and Mary Woodnut, in 1722 m Rachel Craven. His wid., Rachel, m 2d, Daniel Garrison.‖

Joseph, int. 5-17-1735. Rachel Woodnutt, adm.‡

Richard, Salem, bricklayer, inv. 5th of 10th mo. (Dec.), 1688. Wf. Grace.§

Richard. Wf. Mary; chd. Joseph, b 7-5-1697; Richard, b 12-22-1700; Grace, b 5-8-1703; Sarah, b 6-10-1708.†

Richard, Maninton, bricklayer, will 12-30-1726, pr. 2-12-1726/7. Wf. Grace; chd. Joseph, Richard, Grace, who has 2 daus; and Sarah ‡

Richard. Wf. Ann; chd Jonathan, b 3-17-1731; Henry, b 12-14-1735 6 †

Richard, Mannington, bricklayer, will 1-20-1738, pr. 2-21-1738. Wf. Ann; chd. Jonathan and Henry (both under age); sister Sarah, wf. of William Burroughs, mariner.‡

Woodroofe, Joseph, Salem, adm. granted 6-10-1709.**

Thomas, s of John, b in Parish of Cowly, Costiwould Hill, Co. Gloucester, Eng., m Edith, dau. of Joseph Pitt, of Weymouth, Dorsetshire; re. to London, where they had chd. Thomas; Edith, John and Isaac. In 1678, with wf., chd., and maid, Alice, dau. of Leonard Harvey, of Weymouth, re. to West Jersey in the "Success," ar. at Salem in April, 1679. Dau. Mary born at sea.†

Thomas, Salem, will 8-17-1699, pr. 3-2-1703/4. Sons Joseph and John; daughters deceased.§

Wooley, John, mariner, bond of adm. 4-6-1725.‡

Wooleyson (Ouleson), **Peter,** Boughton, planter, will 4-19-1691; rec. 5-18-1692. Chd. Lausey Peterson, Hendrick Peterson, Wooley Peterson, Breeta, Gartre, Karey and Maidlen.§

Peter, inv. 4-2-1687. His wid. m Henry Daniellson.§

Woolsey, John. Wf. Barsheba, Deerfield. Chd. Israel Wharton, bap. 8-30-1741; Benjamin, bap. 10-31-1742.*

Worgan, Richard, Alloways Creek, cooper, will 9-12-1681, rec. 5-22-1682. Wf. Cecelia.§

Worledge, John, m Ann Lefever, 11-6-1684.¶

Worlidge, John, Salem, will 8-2-1698, rec. 2-28-1699/1700. Wf. Ann; chd. not named.§

Joseph, Salem Town, cordwainer, will 3-27-1734, pr. 4-13-1734. Wf. Arcadia; chd. John and Joseph (both under age).‡

Worthington, Ephraim, Pilesgrove, inv. 6-14-1727. Wf. Elizabeth.**

Wright, Jonathan, Elsenburg, inv. 5-22-1716. Ann Wright, adm.‡
Nathan, int 2-20-1724/5. Wf. Sarah.‡
Thomas, will 1-11-1744/5, pr. 4-19-1745. Wf. Elizabeth; chd. Nathan and Joseph.‡
William, int. 9-22-1744. Wf. Desire.‡
William, Stowe Creek, will 12-9-1705, pr. 3-18-1705/6. Chd. John, Daniel, Thomas, Jonathan and William.‡

Wyat, Bartholomew, Mannington Precinct, will 4-21-1726, pr. 1-6-1726/7. Wf. Sarah; s Bartholomew; bros. Henry Wyat, who has s Thomas; and Thomas Wyat, who has s Robert and Thomas; sister Tamson Wilkins, who has s Bartholomew.‡

Bartholomew, emig about 1690. Wf. Sarah; chd. Bartholomew, b 4th of 1st mo., 1697; Elizabeth, b 1706.∥

Bartholomew, s of Bartholomew and Sarah, m about 1730, Eliza-

Tomlinson, b in 1706. Chd. Bartholomew, b 1731; and Sarah, b 1733, m Richard Wistar.‖

Wynckoop, Henry, int. 3-15-1738/9. Sarah Wynckoop, adm.§

Yard, Thomas, Cohansey, inv. 6-10-1695. Wf. Ann.§

Young, John, Mannington Precinct, will 2-10-1727/8, pr. 3-12-1727/8. Wf. Elice.‡

Yourison, Lawrence, Penns Neck, int. 3-1-1750/1. Wf. Mary.§

CORRECTIONS

Page 12, line 41—1-29-1660 should read 1-29-1690.
Page 15, line 28—12-3-1847 should read 12-3-1748.
Page 15, line 32—4-16-1623 should read 4-16-1723.
Page 18, line 27—1-281-733 should read 1-28-1733.
Page 19, line 3—11-15-1682 should read 11-15-1692.
Page 19, line 17—7-15-4691 should read 7-15-1691.
Page 21, line 15—8 12-2704 should read 8-12-1704.
Page 21, line 22—12-4-1657 should read 12-4-1757.
Page 24, line 27, John should read Joseph.
Page 24, line 28—5-29-1747 should read 12-12-1732.
Page 26, line 7—2-17-1944 should read 2-17-1644.
Page 27, line 26—2-19-1927/8 should read 2-19-1727/8.
Page 28, line 24—4-16-1784 should read 4-16-1684.
Page 29, line 19—Mary Bennett should read Mary Burnett.
Page 29, line 20—5-6-1885 should read 5-6-1685.
Page 38, line 11—7-21-1793/4 should read 7-21-1693/4.
Page 44, line 27—11-5-1135 should read 11-5-1735.
Page 45, line 9—10-4-1730 should read 10-4 1708.
Page 51, line 39—3-8-1725 should read 3-8-1728.
Page 52, line 2—3-16-4702 3 should read 3-16-1702 3.
Page 53, line 8—3-20-1799 1700 should read 3-20-1699/1700.
Page 53, line 38—Griffith should read Griffin. (The Salem Friends' Records give Griffin as the name of this vessel, while Cushing & Sheppard and some others call it the Griffith).
Page 55, line 24—4-20-1744 should read 4-20-1714.
Page 58, line 32 Griffith should read Griffin.
Page 59, line 4—7-20-1597 should read 7-20-1697.
Page 59, line 22—Sora, b 12-5-1740 should read Sarah, b 12-5-1721.
Page 68, lines 1 and 35—Griffith should read Griffin.

INDEX

Persons, Other than of Family Name, Mentioned in the Body of this Data

Abbott, Elizabeth, Page 53; Mary, 53, 77; Rachel, 53, 63; Rebecca, 13, 77; Ruth, 65; William, 77.
Adams, Ann, 28; Elizabeth, 28; Fenwick, 13, 28; Mary, 28, 42; Walter, 28.
Alderman, Daniel, 6; Mary, 6; Thomas, 6; William, 6.
Alexander, Thomas, 6.
Alin, John, 40; Mary, 40.
Allen, David, 74, 75; Jedediah, Jr., 16; Rebecca, 74, 75.
Allin, Samuel, 6; Thomas, 6.
Ashbury, Hannah, 68, 83.
Atkinson, Ann, 43.
Aurey, Mary, 37.

Bacon, Elizabeth, 24, 73; John, 24, 32, 69; Nathaniel, 61.
Bagley, Charles, 20.
Bagnall, Ellinor, 60.
Baitman, Sarah, 29; Thomas, 29.
Baker, Jeremiah, 9.
Barber, Aquilla, 33, Elinor, 32, Elizabeth, 21 34.
Barker, James, 79; Wade, 71; William, 34
Barn, Barbara, 46.
Barnes, Elinor, 44; Samuel, 44.
Barracliff, Ann, 79; John, 79.
Barrar, Zachariah, 28.
Barrett, Abigail, 66; Caleb, 66.
Bassett, Abigail, 23, 69; Elisha, 69; Elizabeth, 45; Sarah, 69, 70.
Batty, Jael, 52; Richard, 52.
Beard, George, 21; John, 53.
Bedient, Abigail, 80; John, 80.

89

Beesley, Hannah, 79; Maurice, 79.
Beetle, Ester, 82; George, 21, 82; John, 21; Joseph, 21; Sarah, 21.
Belles, Mathias, 83.
Belton, Lydomia, 25.
Bennett, Hannah, 31; Mary, 29; Priscilla, 29; Rachel, 10; Thomas, 29.
Berry, Thomas, 61.
Besby, Virgin, 20.
Biddle, Hester, 82; John, 83.
Bishop, Sarah, 55;
Biskar, Isaac, 15.
Blackfield, Peter, 21.
Blancher, Elizabeth, 48.
Boerd, Marey, 16.
Bonewell, Robert, 18
Boon, Peter, 19.
Booth, Elizabeth, 41, 53; Margaret, 85.
Bowen, Samuel, 13.
Bowin, Dan, 80; Hannah, 39, Mary, 80; Samuel, 82.
Bowring, Mary, 80.
Brading, Nathaniel, 13.
Bradway, David, 12; Edward, 19, 72, 79; Edward, Jr., 45; Elizabeth, 45, 79; Jonathan, 79; Mary, 72; Prudence, 8.
Braithwaite, Mary, 30
Brick, Ann, 60; Elizabeth, 60; John, 23, 60; Rachel, 27; William, 27.
Brooks, Ann, 15.
Brown, Catrin, 43; Hannah, 76; Thomas, 18.
Buck, Hannah, 65; Ruth, 82.
Buckley, Thomas, 27.
Budd, James, 25.
Bull, Dorothy, 19.
Burden, Mary, 46.
Burkell, Francis, 12.
Burnham, Elizabeth, 48; Ralph, 48; Richard, 48.
Burroughs, Sarah, 56, 85; William, 56, 85.
Burrows, Priscilla, 11.
Burton, John, 79.
Busse, Margaret, 43; Paul, 43.
Butcher, Jane, 21, Job, 63; Richard, 37, 63; Thomas, 63.
Butler, Jane, 47; Margaret, 42.
Butterworth, Catherine, 19; Elinor, 19.

Cairle, Elizabeth, 13;
Camell, Elizabeth, 25.
Cammell, Robert, 66.
Carell, Abiel, 65.
Carman, Margaret, 26
Casperson, Elizabeth, 48.
Chambless, Mabel, 36.
Champneys, John, 28; Mary, 28, 36; Nathaniel, Jr., 79; Nathaniel, Sr., 36.
Chandler, Christian, 60; Mary, 36.
Chard, Hugh, 53.
Chatfield, Anna, 66; John, 66.
Church, Arthur, 83; Elizabeth, 83.
Clark, Ann, 37; William, 12.
Clefton, Elizabeth, 56; Hugh, 56.
Clement, Elizabeth, 62; Joseph, 13; Sarah, 35; Thomas, 62.
Clemont, Mary, 75.
Clifton, Hugh, 11.
Coffen, Lurane, 81.
Collier, John, 51; Sarah, 51.
Coltson, George, 54; Hannah, 54.
Colyer, Mary, 82.
Conchton, Bridget, 62.
Condon, Mary, 74; Rains, 35.
Conkelyn, Phebe, 76.
Cook, Hannah, 73.
Cooper, William, 14
Corneliuson, Cornelius, 11.
Cox, Mary, 82; Rebecca, 38
Craford, Elizabeth, 55.
Crafts, Christopher, 68; Martha, 68.
Craig, Ann, 73.
Craven, Ann, 62; Rachel, 85; Thomas, 8, 68.
Crawley, Eleanor, 23; William, 23.
Cripps, Samuel, 83.
Crocker, Ann, 59.
Crow, Elisha, 62; George, 70; Mary, 70; William, 70.
Cunningham, Abraham, 47.
Curtice, Samuel, 25, 37.
Curtis, Ann, 59.
Curtise, Samuel, 10.
Custolow, Ponthenia, 59.

Daily, Frances, 73.
Dalbo, Catherine, 21.
Daniels, James, 63; Jonathan, Sr., 12; Rebeckah, 72; Ruth, 63.
Darby, Bridget, 46.
Dare, Benoni, 5; Rachel, 13.
Darkin, Ann, 56; Hannah, 49, 83; Jael, 29, 83; John, 83; Joseph, 49, 56, 83; Richard, 83; Sarah, 41, 49.
Daues, Larance, 33.
Davis, Charity, 11; Dorothea, 9; Dorothy, 84; Elizabeth, 52; John, 9.
Dayton, Hannah, 63.
Defoss, Margaret, 6.
Denn, Daniel, 21; Elizabeth, 54, 76; Hannah, 19; James, 48, 54; John Maddox, 48, 76; Margaret, 48, 54; Naomi, 76.
Dennes, Charles, 80; Rachel, 80.
Dennis, Philip, 29; Rachel, 22, 56; Sarah, 29, 54, 56, 69.
Denny, Deborah, 18; Thomas, 18.
Devall, Ann, 36.
Dickey, Jean, 43 Margaret, 29; Mary, 54; Robert, 43.
Dickinson, Sarah, 51.
Dickson, Rachel, 38.
Dixon, Hester, 36; James, 11; Mary Ann, 82; Penticost, 36.
Domony, Elizabeth, 7; Nathaniel, 7.
DuBois, Catharine, 27.
Dun, Ester, 13.

Eaton, Ann, 45.
Edwards, Thomas, 23.
Elger, Marcus, 20.
Elmer, Buhanna, 23; Margaret, 48.
Elmore, Abigail, 47; Daniel, 47.
Elweel, Elizabeth, 40.
Elwell, Joseph, 42; Katherine, 25; Mary, 20, 42; Phebe, 53; Rachel, 70; Sarah, 78.
England, Sarah, 6.
Enloes, Catren, 16.
Erys, Benjamin, Jr , 7; Clemens, 7; William, 7.
Ettenridge, Rebecca, 84.
Euartson, Allderix, 6.
Evance, Mary, 27.
Evans, Gwen, 83; Mary, 58.

Fenwick, John, 5, 26, 38; Capt. Ralfe, 28; Roger, 28.
Fetters, Mary, 17.

Field, Mary, 8.
Fisher, Catharine, 51; Elizabeth, 29; Henry, 29; Sarah, 29, 47.
Fogg, Charles, 51; Daniel, 51; Hannah, 51; Joseph, 39.
Foster, Amy, 5; Ann, 22; Ephraim, 82; Hannah, 5; Joanna, 82; Josiah, 5; Sarah, 82.

Gabitas, Deborah, 34.
Gambell, Elizabeth, 32.
Garm, John, 7.
Garrison, Catherine, 61.
Gelaspse, Rebecca, 63.
Goff, Martha, 80.
Gibson, Elizabeth, 74.
Giljohnson, Ales, 27.
Gilljohnson, Erick, 32; Gilljohn, 38; Rhina, 32; Thomas, 50; William, 58; Yelious, 58.
Gillman, Ann, 7.
Gilman, David, 66; Hannah, 65.
Goodwin, Frances, 18; Mary, 52; Sarah, 52, 69; Thomas, 52; William, 52.
Goose, Elizabeth, 16.
Grant, Alexander, 44; Anna, 44.
Gregory, Elizabeth, 8; Hannah, 79; Renier, 79.
Griscom, Andrew, 24; Elizabeth, 24; William, 24.
Groome, William, 12.
Grover, Mary, 44.

Hall, Ann, 64; Elizabeth, 18, 58; Mary, 83; Nathaniel, 13; Sarah 12; William, 58, 59.
Halton, Elizabeth, 46; James, 46.
Hanbe, Mary, 56.
Hancock, Job, 54; John, 17; Margaret, 7; Sarah, 13; William, 17.
Harding, Elizabeth, 56.
Harris, Josiah, 82; Ruth, 82; Sarah, 44; Thomas, 62.
Harrison, Hester, 83; Joseph, 83; Sarah, 83.
Hart, John, 52.
Harvey, Alice, 86.
Hays, Abigail, 62.
Hea, Margaret, 15.
Hedge, Ann, 28, 33; Anne, 32; Rebecca, 68, 69; Samuel, 28; Samuel F., 68; Samuel, Jr., 28; Samuel, Sr., 40.
Hendricks, Albert, 65.
Hendrickson, Lause, 56.
Henry, Athey, 59.

Hewit, Ann, 46.
Hill, Agnes, 41; Elizabeth, 5; Joseph, 41; Sarah, 74.
Hodge, Joseph, 73; Mary, 66.
Hogben, Elizabeth, 70; John, 68; Sarah, 47.
Hogbin, Elizabeth, 26.
Hoggbon, Neihemia, 11.
Hollingshead, Sarah, 8.
Holme, Hannah, 39.
Holmes, Jona, 7; Jonathan, 51; Suanna, 51.
Hooten, Thomas, 48.
Horsley, Mary, 59.
Hosier, Hannah, 22.
Huckings, Mary, 6; Susanna, 31.
Hudson, Ann, 85.
Hudgins, Roger, 17.
Huggins, Sarah, 34.
Hughs, Elizabeth, 57.
Huings, Sarah, 27.
Huitt, Mary, 70; Randal, 70.
Humbles, Jane, 74; Thomas, 74.
Hunt, Ann, 60.
Hunter, Ann, 26; Samuel, 39.
Hurley, Sarah, 50, 59.
Hutchings, Sarah, 32.
Hutchinson, James, 27; Mary, 57.
Hutson, William, 18.

Jaffrey, Alexander, 42.
Jansen, Margaret, 25.
Jean, Mary, 8; Elizabeth, 8.
Jenkins, Elinor, 44.
Jessup, Mary, 21.
Johns, Margaret, 22; Thomas, 22.
Johnson, Ann, 34, 46, 63; Annabel, 10; Edward, 46; Elizabeth, 24; Eric, 32; Katherine, 84; Martin, 78; Mary, 29; Rebecca, 60; Richard, 56; Robert, 56, 63.
Jones, Anne, 70; Benjamin, 70; Gartheret, 27; Jerusha, 70; John, 70; Lydia, 70; Rachel, 27, 70; Standford, 70.
Jordan, Hannah, 50.

Keasbey, Bradway, 79; Edward, 68; Jane, 79.
Kent, Ann, 57.
Kenton, Mary, 12.
Key, Rebecca, 83.

Kingsber, Jonathan, 14.
Knox, Katherine, 6.

Lacroy, Margaret, 57.
Lambson, Matthias, 42.
Lawrence, Elizabeth, 31.
Lefever, Ann, 86.
Lewis, Ellenor, 30; Esther, 79; Samuel, 79.
Leonard, James, 75; Sarah, 28; Thomas, 28.
Lock, Beata, 18.
Long, Mary, 56.
Loper, Patience, 37.
Lord, Elizabeth, 32; John, 47; Susannah, 6.
Lorence, Elizabeth, 78.
Loyd, Elizabeth, 83; Joseph, 47.
Ludlam, Anthony, 8; Patience, 8.
Lumley, Abigail, 50.
Lummus, Abigail, 82.
Lupton, Mary, 10; Sarah, 9.

Maddox, Elizabeth, 23; James, 23.
Mahu, Joan, 70; John, 70.
Marcy, Edward, 68; Susannah, 68.
Marshall, Elizabeth, 49; Humphrey, 73; Isabel, 73
Martin, Sarah, 81.
Mason, Ann, 77; Elizabeth, 39; Isabel, 30; James, 53; John, 56; John, Jr., 80; Mary, 59; Rebeckah, 56; Samuel, 39; Sarah, 39.
Mathiason, Annake, 53; Israel, 53; Mathias, 53.
Matson, Andrew, 77.
McCarty, Elizabeth, 16.
McClung, Agness, 11.
McGoogan, Margaret, 34.
McKnight, Hannah, 50; Jane, 16; John, 55; Rebecah, 58.
McMungall, Esther, 11.
Mecum, William, 78.
Middleton, Hugh, 12, 83; Mary, 12.
Miller, Hannah, 30; Isaac, 9; Noah, 40.
Moore, Elizabeth, 56; Moses, 56; Nicholas, 40.
Morgan, Isaac, 23; Mary; 20; Rachel, 23; Samuel, 23.
Morris, David, 83; Grace, 56; Jane, 46; Joseph, 35; Lewis, 33, 56; Margaret, 35; Prudence, 35; Sarah, 33.
Morrison, Elinor, 19.
Morton, Samuel, 60; Sarah, 60.
Moss, Abraham, 48; Isaac, 48; Rebeckah, 48; Richard, 48; Thomas, 48.

Mulford, Christian, 63.
Mullicka, Annicka, 47.
Mullin, Ann, 44.
Murfy, Daniel, 32.
Murphy, Eleanor, 25; Margaret, 32; Thomas, 25.

Nealy, Elizabeth, 11; John, 11; Joseph, 11.
Nelson, Hannah, 23.
Newkirk, Janette, 25.
Nicholas, John, 81.
Nicholds, Mary, 6.
Nicholson, Abel, 13, 22, 77; John, 22; Mary, 13; 77.
Nickson, Mary, 84.

Oads, Thomas, 48.
Oakford, Charles, 23, 55; Charles, Jr., 12; Elizabeth, 23, 55; Hannah, 19; John, 55; Wade, 17; Wade Samuel, 55.
Ogden, Hannah, 21; Sarah, 23, 37; Thomas, 37.

Page, John, 9, 66.
Pagett, Dorothy, 63; Thomas, 63.
Paulin, Henry, 70; Patience, 65; William, 65, 70.
Paullin, Josiah, 27.
Pawlson, Catherine, 70.
Pedrick, Elizabeth, 72; Mary, 41; Sarah, 47; Thomas, 72
Pennington, Elenor, 46.
Penton, Caterine, 35.
Percel, Rachel, 82.
Perkins, Elizabeth, 71.
Peterson, Abijah, 39; Catherin, 59; Christiana, 27; Hendrick, 86; Lausey, 86; Lucas, 53; Margaret, 19; Mary, 39; Peter, 67; Purple, 59. Wooley, 86.
Pettey, Israel, 63.
Philpot, Elizabeth, 27.
Pierson, Elizabeth, 44; John 44.
Pitt, Edith, 86; Joseph, 86.
Pittman, Rebecca, 54.
Platts, Mary, 63.
Pledger, John, Jr., 63; Mary, 28, 60, 63.
Plumsead, Clement, 35.
Plumstead, Clement, 35; William, 35.
Plummer, Hannah, 63.
Pope, Margaret, 23.
Powell, Elizabeth, 48; Jeremiah, 10; Mary, 20, 48; Uesty, 6.
Prague, Elizabeth, 39.

Preston, Abigail, 37; Elizabeth, 21; Hannah, 44; Hester, 22.
Prior, Hannah, 44.
Proctor, Hannah, 16; John, 16.
Pyle, Elizabeth, 35; Thomas, 35.

Ramsey, Ruth, 13.
Ray, John, 27; Susanna, 27; William, 27.
Redstreak, Elizabeth, 16.
Redstreicke, John, 58; Joseph, 58; Pledger, 58.
Reeve, Benjamin, 13; John, 13; Martha, 13; Mark, 26.
Reeves, John, 27; Joseph, 27; Mark, 27; Martha, 27; Parthenia, 10.
Remington, John, 61; William, 85.
Richman, Ann, 54; Mary, 64.
Richmond, Henry, 27.
Robbins, Obadiah, 40.
Roberts, Lydia, 16.
Robeson, Ann, 36.
Robinson, Elizabeth, 73.
Rodgers, Mary, 34.
Roland, Sarah, 35.
Rolph, Widow, 12.
Ross, David, 62; Sarah, 62.
Rumsey, Daniel, 70; Ruth, 70.
Russell, Phebe, 56.

Sakel, Eve, 66.
Savoy, Catherin, 11.
Sayer, Mary, 30.
Sayre, Ephraim, 76; James, 8; Joseph, 44; Margaret, 44; Ruth, 43; Sarah, 8; Thomas, Jr., 56.
Scull, Rebecca, 57.
Sears, Joseph, 43; Richard, 43.
Seeley, Hannah; 29.
Sharp, Isaac, 39, 49; Joseph, 89.
Shaw, Joshua, 65; Mary, 39; Nathan, 31.
Shephard, Elizabeth, 47.
Shepherd, Dickason, 5; Mary, 55; Rachel, 81; Samuel, 55.
Sherron, Mary, 72; Roger, 72.
Shirgeon, Abigail, 55.
Shivers, Rachel, 60.
Short, Elinor, 26; Margaret, 53.
Siddons, Joseph, 58.
Sikes, Hester, 40.
Silver, Jane, 15.

Simmons, Elizabeth, 29, 83.
Sinick, Sinickson, 10.
Sinnickson, Andrew, 32; Sarah, 32; Sinnick, 12, 67.
Skeen, Katherine, 41.
Smart, Elizabeth, 45, 73; Isaac, 22, 45, 54, 73; Margaret, 54.
Smith, Ann, 44; Daniel, 60; David, 17; Deborah, 72; Dorcas, 38; Elizabeth, 29; Jane, 79; Jean, 39; John, 12, 33; Mary, 49, 56; Miriam, 70; Rebecca, 38; Richard, 53; Samuel, 31; Susannah, 33; Temperance 60; Thomas, 9; 70, 79; William, 11, 17, 56.
Smithey, Francis, 79.
Snecks, Bridgitta, 30.
Stacy, George, 32.
Staekop, Catrain, 19
Stalcup, John, 27.
Steele, Margate, 15.
Stewart, John, 79; Joseph, 77; Mary, 77, 79; Samuel, 77.
Stratton, Mary, 51; Phebe, 29; Thomas, 51; William, 29.
Stretch, Bradway, 8; Joseph, Jr., 36; Sarah, 8.
Stubbins, Henry, 20.
Stubens, Samuel, 55.
Stubings, Elizabeth, 28; Henry, 28.
Stubins, Henry, 75; Samuel, 75.
Syckes, Henry, 84; James, 84.
Symms, Elizabeth, 79; John, 79.

Taylor, Rachel, 75.
Test, John, 42; Joseph, 42; Mary, 42; Samuel, 75.
Thompson, Andrew, 45, 54 68; Editha, 77; Elizabeth, 68, 77; Isabella, 45, 68; Jael, 22; John, 13, 28, 33, 35, 76; John, Jr., 48; Joseph, 77; Martha, 51; Mary, 61, 76; Samuel, 77; Sarah, 22, 28, 77; Thomas, 22.
Tomlinson, Elizabeth, 87; Joseph, 79; Lydia, 79.
Tomson, Abigail, 52.
Tosaway, Andrew, 78; Thomas, 78.
Townsend, Robert, 77.
Trenchard, Edward, 21, 59; George, 59; George, Jr., 21; George, Sr., 21; Joan, 21; Jona, 59.
Turner, Ann, 36.
Tussey, Sarah, 19.
Tyler, Edith, 74; Joanna, 53; Mary, 53; William, 53, 74.

Vance, James, 57; Mary, 57; Tamsun, 63.
VanHyst, Rennere, 32; Rinier 62.
Vaniman, William, 64.

Vanmeter, Elizabeth, 34.
Vial, Hannah, 78.
Vickery, Mary, 72.

Waddington, Jonathan, 12; Joseph, 63.
Wade, Edward, 80; Hannah, 34, 60; Joseph, 60; Mary, 71; Milicent, 60.
Wagstafe, Sarah, 48.
Waithman, Elizabeth, 21; John, 21; Thomas, 21; William, 21.
Walker, Anne, 47
Wallen, Sarah, 7.
Walford, Hannah, 7.
Walling, John, 11; Sarah, 6.
Ward, Abigail, 25.
Ware, Elizabeth, 73; Joseph, 10, 73, 79; Mary, 56; Sarah, 72.
Watkins, Anne, 5.
Watson, Elizabeth, 76; Robert, 8.
Weaten, Rachel, 41.
Weatherby, Edmund, 58; Martha, 58; Sarah, 6.
Weed, James, 82.
Westcott, Rachel, 21; Sarah, 21.
Wheaton, Elizabeth, 26; Hannah, 81.
White, Christopher 6, 13, 37; Esther, 37; Elizabeth, 69; Hannah, 9; John, 69; Josiah, 9.
Whitehall, John, 17.
Whitten, Joseph, 22.
Whitton, James, 22; Sarah, 22.
Wick, Temperance, 8.
Widdish, Lucretia, 53.
Wieat, John, 82.
Wigorvie, Margaret, 64.
Wilke, Jean, 59.
Wilkins, Bartholomew, 86; Tamson, 86.
Williams, Edward, 83; Jane, 83; Mercy, 73; Nathaniel 80; William, 80.
Willis, Lydia, 67.
Willson, Elizabeth, 76.
Winsor, Solloman, 28.
Winton, John, 27, 80.
Wistar, Richard, 87; Sarah, 87.
Woldin, Mary, 50.
Womsley, Jonathan, 34; Rachel, 34.
Wood, Gabriel, 11, 56; John, 46; Margaret, 11; Martha, 49; Mary

46, 56; Richard, 7; Ruth, 51; Sarah, 74.
  Woodhouse, Mary, 60.
  Woodnut, Henry, 34; Jonathan, 34; Mary, 74; Richard, 74.
  Worldln, Mary, 50.
  Worlidge, Ann, 13; John, 13, 46.
  Wossley, Sarah, 74.
  Worthington, Elizabeth, 26.
  Wright, Jane, 52; Ruth, 46.
  Wyat, Sarah, 22.
  Wyatt, Bartholomew, 84; Sarah, 84.
  Wyeth, Hannah, 53; Joseph, 53.
  Wyncoop, Rachel, 65.

  Yearians, Erick, 56; Stephen, 56.
  Young, Susan, 29.
  Yuens, Maskell, 49.

www.ingramcontent.com/pod-product-compliance
Lightning Source LLC
LaVergne TN
LVHW091603060526
838200LV00036B/983